THE JOY OF HATE

THE
JOY
OF
HATE

How to Triumph over Whiners
in the Age of Phony Outrage

GREG GUTFELD

CROWN
FORUM
NEW YORK

Published in the United States by Crown Forum, an imprint of the
Crown Publishing Group, a division of Random House, Inc., New York.
www.crownforum.com

CROWN FORUM with colophon is a registered trademark of
Random House, Inc.

Library of Congress Cataloging-in-Publication Data

Gutfeld, Greg.
   The joy of hate : how to triumph over whiners in the age of
phony outrage / Greg Gutfeld.
       p. cm.
1. Liberalism—United States—Humor.   2. Political correctness—United
States—Humor.   3. United States—Politics and government—Humor.
4. Political participation—United States—Humor.   5. Patriotism—United
States—Humor.   I. Title.
   PN6231.L47.G88 2012
   808.87—dc23

                        2012026440

ISBN 978-0-307-98696-2
eISBN 978-0-307-98697-9

PRINTED IN THE UNITED STATES OF AMERICA

Jacket photography: © Victoria Janashvili

10

First Edition

Dedicated to Andrew Breitbart

CONTENTS

AUTHOR'S NOTE

All opinions expressed in this book are my own, and nobody else's. So don't blame others for my churlishness. I take full responsibility for any outrage caused. And for those of you who are new to my work, and find it reprehensible, remember that I've done nothing to hide who I am, or what I'm about. Enjoy!

INTRODUCTION

You know what really pisses me off? People who are always pissed off. Or pretend to be pissed off. We've created a new, frantic world of the enraged, the phony grievance, the manufactured outrage. If you make fun of something or say something truthful, someone, somewhere will be unhappy. Or say they're unhappy, even when they're not. When they're bored. When they're lonely. When they need attention. They come for you, whining, crying, screaming. And they are coming for you—the children of the corn, with a platform.

This new rising tide of constant outrage has been fueled, no doubt, by something called the Internet (which has intensified everything, including my home business selling novelty pumpkins). It has led, along with cable news (where I currently reside), to an apology brigade, comprising shrill scolds who overpopulate both sides of the political spectrum. When Rush Limbaugh says something that thin-skinned tools define as "mean-spirited," sundry CNN talk show guests (most of whom never listen to Rush) demand an apology. When Bill Maher says something considered repugnant toward women, conservative watchdogs organize petitions. Everyone wants everyone else fired. No one rests until they get a scalp of contrition, a symbol of victory revealing to all that you just bested someone you don't like.

Then, of course, everyone moves on to someone else. And it doesn't even matter whether they're truly outraged or not. In fact, it's just physically impossible to be this outraged all the time. You'd pull a muscle or throw your hip out. Still, it goes on—an endless game of political ping-pong—with both sides unaware that they sound almost exactly alike.

The bystanders, however, are different. The media, for the most part, tends to dismiss the "outrage" perpetrated by the left, often dismissing the slurs and smears as the product of "edgy comedy," only because they rabidly agree with whatever's being said. You can make ruthless fun of Michele Bachmann, for the editors of the major newsweeklies think she's nuts, too. Remember the "wild-eyed" *Newsweek* cover? I do, and it still aroused me.

This liberal pass, however, is not afforded to those on the right. If Maher calls someone a slut, the outcry lasts a few days. When Rush says it, the outrage lasts as long as a case of herpes. It flares up and never really goes away (or so they tell me).

But I admit, as well, that there are times I seem angry when I'm really not. Oh, some things piss me off. But in a few minutes, I'll see something fuzzy and huggable, like a cute puppy wearing a leather cap with matching chaps, and I'll forget what I was angry about. But many times I'm angry in the same way I'm happy—it's a biochemical commotion in some excitable part of the brain that can be triggered by anything. It's more about me than the thing that makes me happy, or ticked. If I'm yelling at the TV, chances are it's not the TV's fault. It could be the fact that there isn't a TV there at all, and I've been yelling at a window. I hate windows. I see right through them. (I got that joke from a Bazooka Joe wrapper.)

What I have come to realize, however, is that the people who claim to be angry or upset have a bigger agenda. First, they use the language of outrage to score points against people they don't like, or to make themselves feel important. But manufactured outrage is also the freeway to ideological success—the quickest way to win not only an argument but also a career in academics, political activism, or modern dance. To be aggrieved means you've created an impenetrable wall of "feeling" around you: no one can question you, because you're "outraged." If this book doesn't sell, surely I will be outraged—and I will certainly write a book about that.

I hate the outraged so much, you could say I'm outraged by their outrage. The eternally angry were born from the sixties, cultivated in the seventies, coddled in the eighties, stoked in the nineties. The politically correct didn't die, they all just got agents.

And this new outrage came into being via one phenomenon: tolerance. The idea of tolerance—a seemingly innocuous concept—has now become something else entirely: a way to bludgeon people into shutting up, piping down, and apologizing, when the attacked are often the ones who hold the key to common sense. They speak an unspeakable truth, and they get clobbered by the Truncheon of Tolerance. Tolerance has turned normal people into sheep/parrot hybrids, followers in word and deed—bloating and squawking at everyone in a psychological torment not experienced since Dave Matthews picked up a guitar.

Don't get me wrong. Tolerance is a good thing. It wasn't long ago that a lot of awful things were going on in our country. Blacks were treated as chattel, gays were seen as defective humans, and women couldn't vote (well, that last one might be worth revisiting—just because suffragettes are so sexy). But unlike a lot of countries, America actually changed, eliminating or reducing forms of nastiness that this very young country inherited from other older, nastier places. Remember, racism has been around since there were races. And someone is still selling slaves, right now. (I just rented one off Craigslist. His name is Marco and he's a bodybuilding Capricorn who loves Thai boxing.) Modern slavery can be found in Sudan and Mozambique, so I guess most of America's civil rights activists don't see the point. If it won't get you prime real estate in front of cameras chanting about injustice in America, then why bother.

I also realized that because of tolerance, there are no repercussions for bad behavior. And bad behavior won't just continue, but will accelerate, because the tolerati (a name I have coined to describe those who traffic in this repressive tolerance, and hereby trademark, ensuring my comfortable retirement in Bora-Bora with a small army of half-naked manservants) provide the grease for the wheels. Think of the latest stories on teens beating the crap out of adults at movie theaters, fast food restaurants, and subway stops while people look on. No one wants to call them trash, because—well, that's just hurtful. And hurtful often means, "painfully true."

I believe I have identified an insidious kind of entitlement born from a false sense of victimhood. If you are identified as an offensive party dripping with intolerance, especially in this modern age, then you're powerless. You can be accused of anything and you're guilty. The shoe is now on the other foot, and because I'm a straight male of European descent who smokes and is on a network the left hates, that foot is firmly up my ass. And trust me, it's a matter of time before it goes up yours for one reason or another. Permanently. With a steel-tipped toe.

Which is why I hate phony outrage and the tolerance that breeds it. Hate it with a passion. I hate the tolerati, and I hate the toleratic. The toleratic is a person who claims to tolerate anything until he, she, or it meets a conservative. Tolerati describes a group of toleratics grouped in a social setting, like a murder of annoying crows, nattering vacuous opinions and molesting the gnome in your front yard.

I see our country under attack—not by offensive people like me, but by people who claim to be offended. By people like me. See, nothing offends me more than people who are always offended.

I am referring to people who hear jokes that hurt their feelings, and instead of simply assuming the joke-teller is a jerk, they resort to letter-writing campaigns, and they never spell my name right. I am talking about people who wage war over a comment, yet would never think of addressing real behaviors that actually cause actual problems. Yep, they might yell at you for smoking or joking, but they'd never actually address the guy on the corner selling drugs. (Because then they might die. Or worse, he might be part of an ethnic group, which makes you a racist for even looking at him.) They'll condemn the pope for the silliness of organized religion, but then later they tell us we should understand those who—in the name of religion—want to kill us. They'll order us to "question authority," then they'll parrot the latest left-wing attack blog funded by George Soros. That's the funny thing about tolerance: it's actually an avenue for bad behavior, instead of respect for the good stuff. It's why, in the name of tolerance, there are so many mass murderers in the world running countries. We have now made it a rule to respect those who refuse to respect us.

Right now we live in a world where if someone perceives you as "offensive," they win. Meanwhile, the real offenders get a walk. They can wield the weapon of "tolerance" to protect real scummy behavior. Like any act committed by a radical Islamist or past member of Menudo. (Ricky Martin still has my swim trunks.)

As I have gotten older, I have come to realize how the things normally deemed offensive don't bother me anymore. I'm speaking of sexual acts, explicit lyrics in music, garlic knots, staplers, tweed scarves.

But it's the mundane, everyday acceptance of stupidity that I cannot tolerate. For example, I don't find racist jokes offensive. I just find them . . . racist. And that's helpful. Racist jokes help you identify racists. If you like being around racists, great. If you don't, then leave. So what's offensive to me instead?

Public displays of affection—gay, straight, hermaphroditic, animal. I have a rule: Anything that can be done privately does not need to be performed publicly. It's why I love the gays but I hate their parades. Actually, I hate all parades. Marching to celebrate something you're born as seems silly. (As I write this, St. Patrick's Day is in full bore in Midtown. It's delightful how celebrating a heritage requires you to pick fights with strangers and then pee in a parking garage. The upside—the sea of clover-painted drunks moving in unison—might be the only green energy I've ever seen work.) And what's the point of a parade anyway? A bunch of yahoos who share some affinity, walking in one direction? Who decided this was entertainment? For previous generations, this was called a migration, or more often, refugees fleeing for their lives.

However, Super Bowl parades are warranted, because the team actually achieved something, thanks to billions of well-spent dollars on adults with an affinity for strip clubs and pit bulls. It kills me that people actually objected to parades to welcome our military home from Iraq, but wouldn't make a peep about a parade celebrating Anti-Semitic Dwarves with Lupus. At least it was a very short parade.

Religious judgment. I totally respect religious folks, and it's your club, so you have a right to tell members how to live. But you can't use your doctrine to tell me how to live. It can only influence how you live. If you want to argue that my promiscuity, drug use, and cross-dressing are wrong, go for it. But don't use the Bible to do it. Not only will I not listen, but *I don't have to listen.* You can make coherent moral arguments against my sordid life without religion as your tool. It's more of a challenge—and it's one you should embrace. But all of that that pales when compared with . . .

Religious extremism. People who use their religion as a framework to kill people, simply, are not nice people. Yes, that's quite a stand I'm making, but the idea that people are systematically executed because they don't share your God is beyond barbaric. The fact that there are people in our own country who seem to tolerate that, while being intolerant of a Christian's biblical stance regarding gay marriage, makes me want to leave the United States and go to a more sensible place, like Texas.

There are more things I refuse to tolerate (pretentious music criticism, clove cigarettes, slow-moving ceiling fans, restaurant hostesses who pretend they own the joint, people who walk and text on a crowded sidewalk, Hostess Snowballs, people who drop *subzero* into their conversation when they aren't talking about the Arctic winds, people who bring their own bedroom pillows onto flights, pharmacists who yell out your prescription in front of other customers, Time Warner Cable, Sting's chest hair), but I'll get into that later, in the chapter "Arguments for Capital Punishment." I may not do that chapter, though, because I refuse to tolerate lists. They're lazy. And listy.

At any rate, that will be a short chapter, because this book is, among other things, about how modern tolerance sucks—and how it has become a shield for some of the most loathsome behavior you will ever find. It is a fetishized tolerance that is at the root of every single major political conflict we're experiencing now—from terrorism to climate change, from birth control to the left's weird indifference to large-scale, destructive evil. As opposed to small, lesser evils like obesity. Wherever you go, and whatever you say, there will be somebody nearby with a tolerance meter, gauging your behavior, deeming you either acceptable or evil. And then the faux outrage is unleashed. It's the one-two punch that governs everything we do in public life.

The definition of tolerance should be simple: Just treat people the way you like to be treated—who cares if they're different, as long as you don't bother me about it. My definition of tolerance is simpler: I leave you alone, you leave me alone. Works pretty much all the time. Unless I need to borrow underwear. I have such testy neighbors.

Of course, there's that other kind of tolerance—a capacity to endure stuff, like loud music, red wine, and prescribed medications (within that meaning, I am truly the most tolerant man on earth).

But now tolerance means something much greater—and all-encompassing. It's considered, by dictionary.com (nothing but the best research, people) to be "a fair, objective, and permissive attitude toward those whose opinions, practices, race, religion, nationality, etc. differ from one's own." That's covering all the bases, right? Of course, this definition has a big smiley face all over it. Tolerance is seen as a totally positive thing—the opposite of bigotry, the kind of good behavior that every noble television character expresses in spades. It's how you tell the good guys in a movie.

They're the ones who are nice to the gay character. It's the gist of every after-school special, and behind every one of those old, nauseating "the more you know" public service announcements. It's the modern nag, now hip, thanks to celebrity endorsement. If a sitcom star wants to be more than a sitcom star and land a role in the next Sundance-approved flick, they can simply come out against "hate." Even better: Paint NO HATE on your face and you're instantly afforded extra points on the "caring scale," even if you're an obnoxious, selfish, no-talent jerk when the paint washes off.

Intolerance, on the other hand, is portrayed as bad. In fact, intolerance is so rotten, it cannot be tolerated.

Well, that's not quite true. A funny thing about tolerant people? They're really only tolerant when you agree with them. Suddenly, when they find out you disagree with just one of their assumptions, they become intolerant of you. Which kind of misses the whole point of tolerance, but I'll tackle that later.

Here's the curse of tolerance: the "permissive" part. In effect, the modern tolerance movement has forced millions of open-minded liberals into contortions even well-lubricated, multi-jointed circus performers wouldn't try, no matter how many tequila shots and muscle relaxers you supply. (I have boxes.)

And so, in the following chapters, I will examine how the idea and concept of repressive tolerance and phony outrage infect all parts of life, to the detriment of said life. I will include an examination of tolerance's polluting effect on pop culture (in both music and humor). I will show how it was used to demonize the Tea Party, and how this truly organic protest movement was met with virulent, intolerant animosity from the tolerati left. I have touched on many of these topics on my blogs and articles. Some will sound familiar to you if you watch certain shows I regularly appear on, where some began as monologues or commentary on the stories of the day. Many I will reexamine and expand upon, to show you how tolerance has screwed with our common sense, our political leaders, and our policies here and abroad. And where is tolerance often most destructive and/or annoying? The media. Or rather, the mainstream media, which regularly paints Americans as intolerant while they themselves are truly the guilty party. For they traffic in an elitist, detached bubble where everything normal is viewed as quaint and silly. They tolerate everything but the country that must tolerate their sorry and, most likely, flabby asses.

My goal, then, is to help you fight against these tolerant/intolerant masses and their surplus of manufactured outrage, by supplying you with buckets of joyful intolerance. Because the only solution to this tolerant mess is to lovingly embrace intolerance. Smart intolerance, that is. What we used to call "common sense." We need to replace the idiocy of open-mindedness with happy judgmentalism, and embrace the "narrow" mind that finds pleasure in rejecting stupid ideas, notions, and people. We need to get over the need to be liked by others, especially by countries whose own incompetence requires that their violent, toxic prejudices be ignored. We need to monitor our own outrage, and focus it only on stuff that matters. Most important, we need to be jerks, smart intolerant jerks. (But always possessing good manners, decent hygiene, and the willingness to buy a round. All go a long way to bolster an argument.)

And if there's ever been an expert in being a jerk, that's me. I've spent a twenty-five-year career perfecting the craft of jerkiness—from my days at *Men's Health* (where I penned a precursor to this book, "Be a Jerk"), to my captaining of the reeking battleships of offense known as *Stuff* magazine, and *Maxim UK*. My fervent intolerance became infamous at the launch of the Huffington Post, helping to generate most of their traffic in the early days, when their audience was limited to Arianna's attorneys and Ed Begley Jr. If you happen to catch me hosting a few, mighty successful TV chat fests on cable, then you know I won't pipe down when it comes to current events, pop culture, and of course ambrosia recipes (which I am famous for).

In short, I am the perfect pilot for the Good Ship Intolerance and will gently guide you through a world where tolerance-driven outrage threatens to turn us into weak-willed cowards. Hopefully, by the time you've finished reading this book, you will be safe from harm. Or at the very least, finished with a book.

Note: Some names have been changed to avoid getting my ass kicked by angry friends, exs, and coworkers.

THE JOY OF HATE

THE TOLERANT TADPOLE

BEING A TEENAGER IN THE SEVENTIES can be boiled down to two words: shoulder acne. But also something called "feelings." Feelings, nothing more than feelings. That's what it was all about. For most of us, that decade amounted to one big encounter group, where every day was a reminder that you were really mean, you were an oppressor, and you needed to heed other people's feelings (and then, of course, your own, as a method of important self-discovery). If you didn't cry in front of a group of men with beards, then you hadn't really done anything in life. And there had better be Dan Fogelberg playing in the background.

I have no proof of this (other than having had two normal parents and sets of grandparents), but I get the feeling previous generations would have found the idea of putting feelings before thinking as silly. They had other crap to deal with, like fighting diseases and war. There was also that Depression thing (not the coastal health problem, but the historical period), which, from my research, entailed a lot of young children with dirty faces selling newspapers with the word DEPRESSION above the fold. They must have been annoying. Too bad they were (technically) not edible.

But as a teenager, I was now being taught, by folks with little common sense but a lot of acoustic guitars, about other cultures and how superior they were to ours. The flip side was, of course, how mean the United States was toward the rest of the world, and how mean I was, as a tool of that insidious military-industrial complex. (Note: When I first heard "military-industrial complex," I thought it was the coolest thing. How could that be seen as wrong? A country that prides itself on both the military and its industry has to be awesome. Somehow, we went from having a military-industrial complex to having a complex about our military and industry.)

At school, I learned—by accident, really—how to fake caring. I went to a Jesuit Catholic all-boys high school (the team name: Padres), which might conjure up a repressive atmosphere full of belt beatings, angry elderly priests, and hours dangling from a gym rope in tight red shorts. With the exception of the tight red shorts—a fashion that's stayed with me, incidentally—all of that is false. Most of my instructors were earnest types—students of the sixties, well versed in feelings, interested in opening your mind and your soul (translation: Please smirk whenever Ronald Reagan's name is mentioned). This meant sex ed that went a little too far in some places, and religion classes that dove full force into politics. By the early 1980s, we were speaking less about God and more about Central America. There was stuff going on in El Salvador—which I thought was a *Lucha libre* wrestler—and America surely was at fault. As a student, I edited a school paper devoted to that very idea. I wrote a column called "Frisbee Warfare"—a clever title about importing American values into places where it shouldn't be. Teachers loved it because it showed I had "feelings" about the world that matched theirs.

Not that I was an expert in this stupid crap, but I knew it "felt" right. It must be right—the "cool" teacher likes me! Surely America was big and El Salvador was small, so we had to be the aggressor. The David–Goliath story line drives everything in the media. And why not? People love it when the little guy beats the big guy, even if the big guy is good. Even if the big guy is *you*. If you ask me now what the whole mess was about down there, I'd be lying if I told you I had a clue. But pretending to care got me a pretty good grade, and taught me that liberal teachers were a soft touch. Expressing your feelings, coming from the nexus of manufactured rage and tolerance—this was the thing that paved a way to academic success. (And later, Obama's ascendancy to the presidency.)

It was around that time, in high school, that the idea of nuclear disarmament was gaining momentum across the liberal parts of the nation, and especially California. And so I collected signatures for something called "the nuclear freeze." If you asked me what it was, again, as with most things political, I'd have no clue. You could have convinced me it was something you get off an ice cream truck, or even a Finnish sex act involving a popsicle. I think it actually had something to do with getting a bill passed that would make it illegal to transport nuclear arms on California turf. From a lefty point of view, it's a perfect cause to get behind: after all it's based on the simple romantic notion that all weapons are bad, even if those weapons might protect you from bad people who are busy making the very same weapons to kill you with. But by having those evil weapons, that makes you no better than the bad people who want to kill you. To accept this premise, you must ignore the reality around you—i.e., the fact that what kept our enemies at bay was the fear that we would annihilate them. Because of that fear, we never had to actually push a button. Just having the button was enough. It's like owning a Prius. You don't have to use it. Just having it is the statement. (But this Prius actually had purpose, for it could protect the Western world.)

Did I believe in the nuclear freeze? No. But I believed in getting extra credit. And that's what I would be getting if I collected the signatures. My memory is about as clear as bog mud, but I remember that I could boost my grade (taking a B to a B+, for example) for my religion class if I gathered twenty signatures from in front of St. Gregory's Church on Hacienda Street. You could say I found religion. It helped that I wore a sleeveless half shirt. Like a rat getting its edible pellets, I discovered that fake caring could reap rewards. In this case I'd get a higher GPA, which would ultimately get me into a college, where these liberal assumptions would surely be further reinforced (in my case, Berkeley, home of the Cal Bears and homeless defecators who track their own carbon footprint).

But feeling, instead of thinking, can only get you so far, and sometimes you have to start thinking and abandon feeling. For me, thinking began during a high school debate on nuclear disarmament. I was arguing against mutually assured destruction, again from my heart and not my brain. As I mentioned in my previous book, *The Bible of Unspeakable Truths,* my opponent surgically destroyed my arguments so convincingly that he did one thing generally impossible to do in an argument—he changed my mind. It was then I realized that while playing the well-meaning tolerant individual (in short: liberal) garnered you fans and grades, it didn't matter. In my heart and head I was a fraud.

College, for most of us, was nothing if not an instructional guide to the concept of repressive tolerance. I learned early, from high school, that phony outrage about an issue you do not understand is rewarded, but I saw it in full force when expressed by college students, who were really up on the game. Side by side with their instructors, they made the grade by hitting the streets. And later, Kinkos, to print flyers featuring the key word "oppressive," which could describe their body odor.

At Berkeley, I found myself surrounded by purveyors of repressive tolerance, a group of pointless freaks who might have been the most strident, intolerant automatons I'd ever come across. And it was their tolerance that masked their own fascism—their strident beliefs made opposing beliefs unacceptable. I've said it before: The more caring they were on the street, the less they cared at home. Sure, they worried about the dietary deficiencies of Guatemalen water snakes, but they'd never pay their "fair share" for food. They were the worst roommates in the world. If it was their turn to buy toilet paper, you can bet you'd be on the bowl using pages from *Mother Jones*. (I still use *Mother Jones* for that. The articles by David Corn tickle.)

It was there, at Cal, that I discovered what I could not tolerate. And that was the loudmouth, ultratolerant, shrieking outrage junkies who demanded I think the same. One night, walking home from the library, I came upon a "march" for God knows what. There were a lot of marches at Berkeley in the eighties, and frankly I lost track of causes. It's sort of like a giant incubator where parades gestate. If they weren't about apartheid or homelessness, they were about transgender issues or starving pandas with substance-abuse problems. (I seem to remember Poo-Paw, a panda addicted to crack cocaine who'd fallen on hard times and was now turning tricks in the Chinese province of Gansu. But that's another story for another time. Please remind me when you see me—it'll bring a tear to your eye.) But this particular group was very loud, very female, and so very outraged about everything. On the sidewalk I sank into my jacket as I walked with my books (some "borrowed" from the library), while they chanted

"No means no, no means no" over and over again. I felt their eyes on me. And sure enough they were. (Then again, I was addicted to cough syrup during that sophomore year, so this could all have been a hallucination. I remember spending most of my nights arguing with a poster of Heather Thomas.)

Now, I get the concept "no means no," but you're wasting that precious energy on me. Just to clarify: I'm not a rapist. I've never contended that no means, "Sure." It didn't matter. I was the target of their raging rage machine and I would have no choice but to take it. My no apparently doesn't mean no at all. Anyway, they yelled at me, wild-eyed and gesturing, convincing me to avoid eye contact, speed up to a semi-jog, and scamper through a driveway and up the side stairs of the dilapidated fraternity I called home.

It was at this point in my life that I developed a very simple theory, something I call negative identity formation—or NIF for short. Through NIF, I found out who I really was. Through rejection of an abundance of beliefs, discrimination against earnest ideas, and intolerance of those who were trying too hard to be different, I found out that hate isn't so bad after all.

I mean, without it, where would I be? I would be marching for anything and everything. I'd protest for the sake of protest simply because every issue is the same: just a conduit to express rage as a method to raise my own self-esteem. And so I embraced my own narrow-mindedness, because without it I would have become an amorphous blob, floating through life, incapable of making decisions or even the bed (like most lifelong "activists" who are currently avoided by their relatives). And I realized that by refusing to make concrete, narrowed decisions about your life, you'll be living on the street in a refrigerator box—which isn't a bad thing if that street is, say, on sunny College Avenue, where a bum can cultivate a yearlong lustrous tan. But the bottom line, the overarching idea of intolerance—not liking things—actually makes you a better person. You cannot go through life being tolerant of everything, unless you're Deepak Chopra, who is a living hologram making millions off unhappy people, only to spend it on embarrassing caftans and nervous assistants.

But I want to be clear: Being an intolerant person doesn't mean you wish to impose your beliefs on others. I can hate people but at the same time be completely fine and even encourage them to live whatever life they lead. Fact is: *I don't care.* I don't care, I don't care, I don't care. When a gay man tweets me, saying, "I'm tired of people judging me on my sexuality," my feeling is, Then stop tweeting about it. I don't care if you're gay. I do care, however, if you're an idiot. I hate idiots. Gay or straight. But when it comes to lifestyle choices that cause no harm, have at it. Send me pictures. High-def, preferably.

Gay marriage is a perfect example. I don't believe a human being has a right to tell another human being whom they can love or whom they can marry. At this point you might hear the response, "Well, what's next? People marrying dogs?" Well, if you wanna go there, sure, marry a dog. Some of these little poodles are kind of hot, in a Nicole Richie sort of way. Just pick up the poop after your spouse and I'm okay. My wife does it for me, and we're very happy.

But if I'm running a business, I don't want to pay for your dog's health insurance, even if he is your spouse. So that's where my tolerance ends. Same with polygamists. Sure, marry all the women (or men) you want, but if I'm your boss, I ain't paying all those insurance premiums. I would go bankrupt. So there are limits to tolerance.

Fact is, though I am proudly intolerant, I don't want to have any part in dictating what people do in their bedrooms, or their lives. But I also don't want an activist getting in my face (or in my pants), telling me who I should accept or what I shouldn't. You do no one any favors by screaming at Mormons or Catholics because they think only men and women should marry each other. (How funny is it that gay activists stay away from black churches; it's the same hypocrisy you see with the animal rights group PETA. They'll throw paint on a white guy wearing ostrich boots, but they'd never do that to a Native American strangling a bald eagle to make a feather headdress.)

Organized religion has done a lot of great things for society (in some ways, ensuring that it existed), so bear with the parts you find ridiculous. You're winning that battle anyway. More and more Americans are fine with gay marriage, and I hope in a decade or so I will be able to marry my Pekinese, Captain Furfoot, in a tasteful wedding on the beach. And if you don't tolerate that, fine—I just don't want to hear about it. But I swear it's going to be a great wedding, and I condemn you if you don't allow me to follow my bliss.

People ask me what I am politically, and I've previously offered this equation: I became a conservative by being around liberals. And I became a libertarian by being around conservatives.

So what made me move politically from one side to the other? It wasn't the politics. It was the humor. Or lack thereof. As I hung around more liberals—well-meaning, self-serious, and ultimately annoying—I found them utterly devoid of humor. It was replaced with earnest outrage, most of it cultivated as a method to exercise superiority over their parents and everything they'd worked for all their lives. Leftism = I hate you, Daddy, for being tough. And successful.

I guess I owe my conversion to intolerance, and to Berkeley. I was a good-natured kid when I got there, with good-natured ideals and ready-made politics for that campus. But when I came face-to-face with the "believers," I realized that they lacked one thing that made life enjoyable: they couldn't take a joke. I noticed this at the daily protests on Sproul Plaza, populated by suburban kids who'd just discovered piercings and tie-dye but had not yet embraced independence from their parents' checkbook. They were as funny as hepatitis. With complications.

Over the next three months after that night running into that march, I faced this strident ideology everywhere—from my course-work among deconstructionists, to students who harangued me for being in a fraternity, to a daily college paper that had created its own foreign policy, in which the only enemy was us. Aka the U.S.

One summer, an ex decided to rent a room in my vacated fraternity. I humored myself into thinking there would be an opportunity for a month of rekindled hazy summer sex—but then she called me, telling me how excited she was to come. All she kept saying was how she looked forward to "the vibe," and how Berkeley was "like the coolest most open place ever." That was the warning.

When she arrived, it became clear that she had stopped shaving. She still had the body of a cheerleader, but covered in the mane of a yeti. She was Bigfoot in Birkenstocks.

And her politics made her a perfect fit for this asylum. From afar, not dealing with the daily machinations of Berkeley's corrupt and destructive utopian adventures, she had no idea what would transpire. Within a month, she left town—without paying her rent. And when I cashed her deposit, she threatened that her daddy would sue me. This is how modern feminism culminates. When reality strikes, someone—a daddy in the form of a real one or a government substitute—inevitably must bail you out.

It was around this time something special happened. I found a friend. That friend was a magazine. A fraternity brother of mine was picking up his mail when I saw him grab this oversized glossy-covered magazine (inside, though, the pages were like newsprint, with odd-looking illustrations and weird fonts). I asked him what it was, and he lent me his copy. That night I read *The American Spectator,* and understood almost none of it.

It confused me, because it was funny—and it was poking fun at things you weren't supposed to laugh at. The targets were all liberal icons. What the *Spectator* was committing in my world was sacrilege. My favorite part I didn't even understand at first. It was called "Current Wisdom," and it consisted solely of excerpts from various liberal columnists like Anthony Lewis, and rags like *The Nation.* They ran without comment—as a statement that these ideas are so ridiculous, they require no explanation or joke. That back page turned me into a conservative, when I realized that no one needed to make fun of liberalism. It was hilarious on its own.

This was an epiphany. Probably the only one I ever experienced in my life (if you don't count the incident in Key West that culminated in a series of painful apologies and injections), and it changed me forever. I mean, how do you make fun of something that is already a joke? No wonder leftism gets away with its craziness—no one knew how to write a punch line for a punch line.

I started reading the mag from cover to cover—from Bob Tyrrell's "Continuing Crisis" to the book and movie reviews that seemed light-years ahead of anything I'd find in *The New Yorker.*

Once I "got" it, boy did I get it. I started writing parodies of liberals I knew, and even filmed an amateurish skit called *Poetry and Progressives.* Finally, I was given the key to confront the outrage of the left, and that key was mockery, pure and simple. I wasn't that good at it at first. But it became my bread and butter for the rest of my life.

This happened again, much later in life, when I began to run into young conservatives who, sadly, started adopting the pretensions of their counterparts on the left. The Republican Party was supposed to be the "who gives a shit" party of P. J. O'Rourke, but it was starting to mimic the anger of the left. Part of this came with success. There was an explosion of young conservative bloggers and writers, many of them amazingly funny, others not so much. The angry ones, who forgot the humor, made me wince. They were adopting the voice of perpetual outrage, and it wasn't doing them, or me, any favors. That's how I ended up investigating libertarianism. To me, libertarianism happily rejects the moralism on both sides—the only time it pops up, really, is when you say something negative about Ron Paul. By the way, Ron Paul may be the sexiest presidential candidate with two first names ever, and I dare you to refute that fact without becoming visibly aroused.

MY BIG FAT GAY MUSLIM BAR

MOST NEW YORKERS WILL TELL YOU we have plenty of gay bars. There are three within my block, and one in my shower. Still, I disagree. We needed one more. And so let's hark (how do you "hark," exactly?) back to the summer of 2010, a marvelous time for loudmouths like me, when a controversy bubbled up from the blogs—and downtown Manhattan—all thanks to something called Park51.

It became known through various websites—and then the networks slowly and belligerently followed—that a mosque was going to be built near Ground Zero, the gaping wound New York still has from 9/11, and a reminder that radical Muslims flew planes into our buildings and killed our people.

Understandably, most people thought this mosque idea was a pretty weird thing, to put it mildly. How can any civilized person consider building a mosque so close to a place where nearly thousands of people died at the hands of a select group of radicals who hung out in mosques?

Yeah, we all get the whole freedom-to-practice-your-religion thing—and the fact is, if you want to build that mosque, we can't stop you. That's the intellectual argument and what makes our country so much better than yours ("yours" is directed at anyone reading this book in France).

But the commonsense argument is, Why would you? I mean, it's what people at the bar call a "dick move." Yeah, I'm free to make jokes about 9/11, but I pretty much don't. I know the difference between exercising my freedoms and bad taste. And the mosque, let's face it, is in bad taste, only because they didn't seem at all concerned about bad taste. But I also realize, bad taste is not illegal. If it were, every reality star on Bravo would be on death row.

But of course the moment this anxious sentiment about the mosque was raised, it drew ire from the mainstream media. They called it evidence of intolerance—or rather, Islamophobia. You—the Islamaphobe—don't want the mosque built, obviously, because you hate Muslims. All of them.

I say, No, I don't hate all of them. I just hate the ones who kill us. And the ones who cheer those who kill us. And the ones who don't say anything about the ones who support those who kill us. And the ones who make excuses for them killing us. So yeah, I hate those Muslims. And throw in the non-Muslims who can't bring themselves to see this difference. I hate them more, actually, than the Muslims.

I suppose that makes me intolerant.

Now, this is hilarious. Think about it: Because you hold a sensible opinion that's sensitive to others' emotions about a hugely traumatic event in our collective history, you're a bigot. You're intolerant. It's the kind of thinking that ensures that Gitmo has a state-of-the-art soccer field while your kid's high school holds bake sales in the rain to build one of their own. It's amazing that looking out for those who have suffered, you become the bad guy.

And so there were two key things wrong with the arguments attacking those critical of the mosque.

One, nearly all of the sensible people opposed to the mosque *still understood* that the mosque had every right to be there. We were not questioning whether the "community center" could be built—we were just questioning the wisdom of building it. So that's not intolerance at all. That's just an opinion, and in fact, an incredibly tolerant one. Because you're saying you don't want it there but you wouldn't stop it from being there. That's the true definition of tolerance. Tolerance only matters when it comes to actions and things you don't like. You want to see intolerance? Try to build a Jewish temple in Saudi Arabia's capital. Your entire construction crew would be transformed into kindling before the first shovel hit the soil.

The real intolerance, in effect, was coming from those accusing the rest of us of intolerance. They called us hatemongers. Yet it was those tolerant tools who were refusing to respect, or "tolerate," an opposing opinion. They were the truly intolerant, the narrow-minded, the closed-brained. (And to add insult to injury, they wanted to use public funds to help build it—all in the name of "healing." So you're telling us you want to build this thing to bring the faiths together? You're off to a great start, guys. Why not just produce *UBL: the Musical?* Wait, maybe that's not a bad idea!)

So this got me to thinking: How odd was it that a mosque—which has coddled preachers of hate—was being championed as a beacon of tolerance?

That's when I decided to test the mosque and its defenders. I announced on my blog that I was opening a gay, Islam-friendly bar next to the proposed mosque. I was sincere about this, and I had spoken to folks who were seriously interested in investing.

After I made the announcement, I received, in a matter of days, thousands of offers, ranging from financial advice to actual investment. Actually, the offers of money poured in—from a few bucks to tens of thousands of dollars. It became so overwhelming, I gave up opening my e-mail. I received calls from networks all over the world—from Israel to Istanbul. Old ladies offered me part of their life savings; big-deal investment brokers wanted in on the ground floor (which, sad to say, didn't exist, yet). I received a flood of suggestions for the name of the bar—some enormously clever, others just obscene and stupid. I liked the obscene and stupid ones the best. I'm simple like that.

But during this exercise, I exposed the true lie and hypocrisy behind those planning the mosque. The morning of the day that I was to appear on a major TV show to discuss the gay bar (tentatively titled Suspicious Packages), I made a few phone calls—first to the PR flacks fronting the mosque, the actual developers themselves, and the office of the imam who was heading the mosque project. No one got back to me. I finally found Park51 on Twitter (their handle is the actual street address). And there I asked them, bluntly, if they would support my gay bar.

They replied, "You're free to open whatever you like. If you won't consider the sensibilities of Muslims, you're not going to build dialog."

Bam! They made my point, in one simple sentence: If you won't consider their sensibilities, get lost. This from a member of a group who refused to "consider the sensibilities" of the 9/11 victims' families. The irony was so thick it would take you three tries to behead it with a large saber.

(Note: Because Park51 accused me of not wanting to build "dialog," a friend suggested that I change the name of the bar to Dialog. That way, in effect, I would be building Dialog! Get it? No? Well, I don't like you either.)

And there you realize how far Islamic public relations has come. They've discovered the secret to winning all debates:

hiding behind the shield of repressive tolerance. They were now more American than ever! For they quickly realized they can use "tolerance" as a weapon to subdue even its most polite critics, like me. Here you have a group, led by an imam who implicated the actions of the U.S., in part, for 9/11, calling me insensitive! These guys were learning fast, and I had to hand it to them. From the seventh century all the way to the twenty-first! How long until they cut a reality show deal? Or an album with the Dixie Chicks? The secret to blending, they found, was by bleating.

Just so you know, some of the mosque backers think Sharia law ain't so bad. Mind you, Sharia law has no plank in its platform for tolerance—unless that plank is for hitting women over the head with. So in the most surreal mental mindmeld you can imagine, you have a group of intolerant people, open in their disgust of gays, women, atheists, and any religion that isn't theirs, demanding tolerance for their intolerant beliefs. That's balls: To them, tolerance is only a one-way street—the one Theo van Gogh died on. If you don't know him, you should.

Before Park51 realized their Twitter feed was doing them no favors, they started responding to critics flippantly and, in attempts to be "hip," actually poked fun at other religions. Here was one, directed at a guy with "Amish" in his Twitter handle:

Amish saying stop Muslims? 1. What are you doing on the computer? 2. That's not very Amish 3. Shouldn't you be making butter?

This is funny—and possibly a not half-bad haiku, even without the intolerant hypocrisy. The Amish do not use modern technology like Twitter. How awesome is it Park51 had the guts to poke fun at those who aren't even there to fight back?

When I engaged these folks on Twitter, more people found their feed, and the mosqueteers realized their hypocrisy was under scrutiny. So, suddenly, the tweeter disappeared, as did those silly (but no less intolerant) tweets.

Perhaps the mosque boss fired the poor tweeter and sent him home. Which, to me, is sad. Because in America, you can—and should—make fun of the Amish. You can make fun of Scientologists, too. And Catholics. This isn't Islamabad, folks. It's Islamagood! If the mosqueteers understood this, they would know that you can also make fun of Muslims. You can even print cartoons about them.

But actually, now that I think about that, I'd be dead wrong about the "making fun of Muslims" part. You can make fun of every religion in the book but Islam. To paraphrase Gavin McInnes, writer and founder of *Vice* magazine, there is a *Piss Christ*. But there's no *Piss Anybody Else*. After all, rich artists prefer bundles of money over beheadings. You can't relax at the Chateau Marmont, sipping champagne and chasing pool boys, without your head. Better to rip on Catholics—they're nice people who obey the law!

To make my point clearer about the gay bar: I was trying to show that if the Muslim faith were truly tolerant, then they would welcome a gay bar. But the point doesn't need to be made clearer—we know they wouldn't—for they hate gays. In some countries they kill them. What I wanted to accomplish, I did: I revealed the fundamental hypocrisy of their "tolerance" defense.

It was too easy.

But more important, I exposed the hypocrisy of the gay left. Here's a test: If a gay man had to choose between a straight, conservative male advocating gay rights, or an intolerant cleric espousing the death of homosexuals, who would he defend?

You would be surprised, for aside from a few gay bloggers and writers, the gays on the left assessed my proposal as "anti-gay." Yep, my idea to open a gay bar was seen as "anti-gay." In effect, my challenge to Islam to face the reality of gay life . . . was perceived as homophobic. And so you witness the shape-shifting nature of tolerance. Leftists would rather be tolerant of people who want them dead than a person fighting for gay acceptance. Why? Well, because that person doing the fighting, isn't a leftist like them. Talk about Stockholm syndrome. Unless being murdered in a fundamentalist pogrom is the latest fad sweeping Manhattan's Chelsea district, I'm just not getting this.

How tolerant is that?

Short answer: not very.

Longer answer: The controversy arising from the Ground Zero mosque provides a beautiful lesson in repressive tolerance. The ploy—protecting intolerant ideas under the shield of tolerance—underlined the surreal nature of the media circus. In the end, it could prove dangerous. With Muslim women now asking to be exempt from security practices while boarding planes, we find that tolerance requires you be treated the same and differently—simultaneously. And the result, a more unsafe world—all in the name of tolerance. I'd call it cartoonish, but that would be insulting to *The Family Circus.* Or *Garfield.* Or even *Brenda Starr.*

Which reminds me. As the mosque controversy exploded, and the media began painting all mosque critics as Islamophobes, newspapers decided to remove a single paneled comic strip from syndication. The cartoon—titled "Where's Mohammed?"—was a parody of "Where's Waldo?" And there was no Mohammed in the cartoon. Still, out of fear, thinly masquerading as tolerance, the editors of the *Washington Post* Style section had it removed. Other papers followed. The irony—that a few in the media labeling citizens as Islamophobes were suddenly acting like moral cowards under the mask of tolerance—tells you everything you need to know about the wussification of modern life. Honestly, spineless hypocrisy like this is why no one's buying papers anymore, and instead would prefer to get their news from a short, loud talk show host with an embarrassing birthmark situated awkwardly above his pelvis.

THE WAR ON MOOBS

THIS IS A CHAPTER ABOUT the male breast. The beautiful, succulent, but often misunderstood, male breast. See, as we become a society overrun by scolds and whiners, we will come across stuff that's deemed evil, when it's not.

Colloqualisms are often the first to get hit. Whether it's "chink in the armor" or perhaps a word like *niggardly,* the easily offended would rather not have such things present in everyday language—even if you're using them correctly and without offense. But for the most part, I get it. These days, I can't believe anyone would use the word *niggardly* in a headline if it wasn't intended to get a snicker from a racist who takes pleasure in the not-so-veiled similarity to the vile slur against blacks. I'll give a pass, however, to Ohio Democratic senator Sherrod Brown, who, when appearing on MSNBC's *The Dylan Ratigan Show* back in March 2012, used the word *niggardly* to describe how some in Congress are acting toward veterans. He used the word correctly, and without malice to blacks. I make this point knowing that an equivalent writer on the left would not give the same pass to a Republican senator who might do the same thing. I guess I am just a better person (I can bench-press twice my own weight and I'm learning Esperanto).

So we'll let that go. My concern, for the moment, is "moobs." Moobs are man boobs. You've probably seen them around town—usually at the public pool, or at the Sandals resort you made the mistake of visiting in the late nineties. Moobs travel in pairs and are often connected to middle-aged men who suntan poorly. Possessors of moobs are generally gentle souls who shun exercise in favor of beer and television. Moobs are a scourge of dudes as they drift into their forties (and also for young, unfortunate men suffering a medical condition called gynecomastia). I had moobs for about three years, when I gave up the gym in England in favor of red wine, Indian food, and training bras. When they became too big—so big, in fact, that I would get aroused by them when I caught myself in the mirror—I realized it was time to return to the toning and firming that I'd performed with relish years before. That's the cruel prank of exercise—all those bench presses I did to give me that hardened V-shape chest were now paying me back in erotic flab. Once you stop pumping iron, that muscle sags like CNN's ratings. It was time to either hit the gym or switch genders.

I bring up moobs for the sake of a man named Eduardo Ibarra Perez, who, back in May 2010, ended up on a most-wanted flyer, shirtless. Perez was wanted for a variety of infractions, but it seemed the most obvious one at the moment was his gigantic moobs. What made them stand out, though, was not their flabbiness but the fact that the flabbiness had been blurred, so you could not make them out. Yes, whoever in law enforcement decided to distribute the flyer felt that Perez's breasts might be too offensive to our puritan sensibilities, perhaps because they so closely resembled the pouting female bosoms of a local female (the similarities to my 1983 prom date were uncanny; oddly, she also ended up on a law enforcement poster).

I could imagine the discussion between the folks who had created the flyer.

"Wow, he has great tits."

"That's got to be a 34C."

Then an administrator probably walked by, fresh from a course in diversity training, thoughtfully stared into the distance for a brief moment, and said, "We can't have that. That's offensive." I'm sure that was met with silence, as everyone in the room thought, "You've got to be kidding me."

Well, whoever was concerned about these tits wasn't kidding, and his repressive tolerance won, because these beautiful hairy breasts were now obscured. And why? Because they looked like something that normally would have been obscured had they actually been, um, that thing. But they weren't. They were male breasts, but because they could be construed (in someone's head) as appearing female, they must be blurred.

And this is the same mentality behind the actions of the modern tolerati. The offense they deem offensive doesn't have to be offensive as long as someone might construe it as offensive. Or rather, miscontrue.

Misconstrued should be the word that defines the modern era. So many things these days are misconstrued, only because the tolerati have blanketed our culture with the potential for taking everything the wrong way. Seriously, how weird do you feel now when you use the phrase "black market" in a sentence when there's a black person nearby? Could it be that a black teen might not have heard that phrase before, and therefore would think you were being racist? Similar stuff has happened.

As reported on the Dallas City Hall blog, back in July 2008, during a meeting concerning how to process Dallas County traffic ticket payments, Commissioner Kenneth Mayfield made a comment about how so much paperwork had been lost in the office. He said, to the horror of others in the meeting, that Central Collections "had become a black hole." Mayfield is white, I should point out—only because Commissioner John Wiley Price, who is black, took it the wrong way. Or rather, misconstrued its meaning. He interrupted Mayfield with an "Excuse me!" and then added that the office had actually become a "white hole." Indicating, more than anything else, that either (a) Price is incredibly thin-skinned and just begging to be outraged, and/or (b) he doesn't actually know what a black hole is. This is the kind of guy who probably blames astrophysics itself for even having black holes. "Black holes? Proof the entire universe is racist!"

You might think I made this whole thing up in my head as a joke, except you can Google it for yourself. And the incident didn't end there. Judge Thomas Jones, who is black, also felt that this phrase "black hole" was deeply insensitive, and demanded an apology from Mayfield. Mayfield defended himself, saying the term was a scientific phrase and a figure of speech. Ironically, the judge seemed to be more bigoted than anyone, assuming no black person would have known what a black hole was. Thankfully, TV cameras caught all of this, and it made national news, and fodder for diminutive freaks like me.

Now, one solution to all this is to have someone present at all times called a Misconstrued Umpire, who hits a buzzer whenever someone takes something the wrong way. One other option would be to never use the phrase "black hole," and instead when you want to use it in a sentence, say something like, "Wow, Tom, your office has turned into the invisible remains of a collapsed star, with a powerful gravitational field in which nothing can ever escape." Sort of like Al Gore.

Or you could just lighten up.

Crap, that's racist—sorry about that.

How about, "You could stop taking this crap so seriously."

This folly of misconstruance (I hope that's a real word) reared its absurd head in the 2012 Summer Olympics, when NBC was forced to apologize over a poorly timed advertisement featuring a monkey doing gymnastics (promoting an upcoming new show about animals). The ad aired right after Gabby Douglas's gold medal win. Douglas is black, so apparently someone believed that NBC had somehow planned all this, thinking, "Hey, let's run this ad with a primate right after a black gymnast wins." This is so idiotic, my fingers are actually vomiting as I type this.

But if there's anyone who is racist, it's the person who registered the initial outrage. After all, if you made the link between a chimp on the rings and the delightful Gabby, aren't you the actual racist? Wasn't that thought in your head and not in NBC's? NBC had no idea, but *you* did. Because no one in their right mind would go out of their way to do something like this. It was a gymnastics-themed ad that was placed among the gymnastics portion of the Olympics. No one thought it through further. Nor should they have.

Yet it was NBC who had to apologize for the perception of racism, not the reality of it. That's like me apologizing for being topless at the beach, simply because my ample cleavage makes you think of Jenny McCarthy circa 1998.

Anyway, back to moobs. Because Eduardo's was a hilarious story, we chose to do it on one of my shows. But as we did more research (i.e., Googling), we found that the guy had a history of domestic violence. Apparently a decade earlier he had told his wife he was going to kill her. Then he shot her in the head. So we decided to shy away from the story, because it's hard to be funny about moobs when they're connected to a monster. Frankly, he'd given moobs a bad name, and moobs had already been through enough. Certainly mine had.

FLUKED FOR LIFE

SHE PREFERRED FREE PILLS over free will. Back in late February 2012 a woman claiming to be a law student, named Sandra Fluke, offered testimony before the House Democratic Steering and Policy Committee. I say she's "claiming" to be a law student because she's so much more. In reality, she's a professional activist, a thirty-year-old woman who has spent her adult life demanding things that the rest of us should pay for. In this case, she was demanding that religious institutions like Georgetown University pay for her (and everyone else's) birth control pills. This was her crusade, and the Democrats welcomed her with open flabby arms. After all, the testimony was happening just as the Obama administration basically was telling the Catholic Church to screw themselves (without protection) with regard to Obamacare. Yep, O's mandated health care had something in there saying contraception, sterilization, and the morning-after pill must be offered free of charge by Catholic-affiliated organizations like colleges, universities, and hospitals. It became an ugly brawl—about religious freedom and tolerance. Can the government force a religious institution to act in a way that their very religion finds objectionable? And so the time was right for Fluke to become a star. And in the age of the tolerati and their obsession with entitlement, she deserved to be. She was the modern mascot of the protracted moan, the Norma Rae of "you will pay."

Fluke had made the claim that during a three-year stint as a law student, you'd be expected to pay up to 3 grand for your pills—comparing that egregious sum to all the wages you'd make from a summer job (which would lead me to suggest to Sandra: Get a better summer job, or maybe just any job).

Forget her math for a second, because it's silly. Pills cost dollars a month, and if you can't afford them, then clearly you are too lazy and stupid to have sex—which is very lazy and stupid indeed. And if you expect us to pay for that, what next? Dinner? The movie? Your eHarmony account? A lot of work goes into having sex, and all of those play an important role in getting it done. I've argued before that even gasoline should be free, for without it, how would you get to the pharmacy to pick up your pills? If a feminist does not demand free fill-ups for her Prius, well, she's just part of the problem.

But look, the real problem was the sense of priority and proportion this issue had assumed. Fluke called having to pay for birth control an "untenable burden." Apparently, she'd never met a girl trying to go to school in Afghanistan without being doused with acid. That's a real burden, and even those who suffer from them might not call them untenable. As the son of a father who died of cancer, I can vouch for this: the last two years were untenable. Needing a wheelchair just to get your mail is untenable. Taking a cocktail of drugs to fend off infections? Untenable. But every Jane with an iPhone and an addiction to Starbucks lattes not being able to have her recreational sex life with beta males fresh from Occupy Wall Street subsidized by you and me, that was even more unacceptable. The fact is, in the age of repressive tolerance, we have to accept everything the left demands, or we will be seen as sexist, bigoted, evil. If you wanted Catholic services to make up their own minds, clearly you were waging "a war against women."

And that's how the left bamboozled everyone, with the help of the compliant media, who bought her spiel—hook, line, and stinker. On your dime.

Fluke was savvy enough to make this not about sex (when that's the only thing it's about) and turned it into a "women's health issue." She put forward one case about a woman (her friend) with an ovarian cyst caused by not being able to get free birth control—yep, one case. And you know if you asked for another, she'd probably have to get back to you. But asking for more examples would only paint you as intolerant, and without a doubt, misogynistic. And pro-cyst.

As a health editor in my younger days, I know you can portray anything as a health issue. Because that's exactly what I did, to fill up the pages of *Prevention* and *Men's Health* every month. If birth control pills are a health concern that must be subsidized, then surely condoms are as well. I should never have to pay for another rubber until I die. Although, like most men, I'd probably only buy one, which would slowly disintegrate in my wallet, becoming pro-phylactic potpourri.

But a bigger concern, if we're talking about making demands, is sex itself. If we must pay for Fluke's pills because they are an "untenable burden," she in turn should pay for my sex life (which is untenable in more ways than I can relate). Research shows that loneliness is a heavy stressor on men. Men who go to bars and come home alone are often depressed and prone to self-destructive behavior. We do know that women live, on average, 10 percent longer than men. And I've said before that sexual rejection syndrome can be at the root of this discrepancy. When men don't get laid, they find other things to do that aren't nearly as fun, or as healthy. Drinking, for example, which leads to increased risk of all sorts of ailments (especially if you get too drunk and fall down a flight of stairs). Men also fight when they're alone, and black eyes and fractured noses are definitely considered a health problem at the emergency room. The doctor will even write "untenable" right across your chart. So by this logic, someone should be buying me hookers to ease my burden, perhaps you (and I prefer brunettes). And what about the consequences of sex with hookers, which is another alternative for a lonely man without a pliant partner? STD treatment can be expensive, too. Do you think that Democratic Steering Committee might hear me out on this?

Forget that health insurance should really only pertain to serious stuff. This sad and stupid debate should be pretty simple: it's between those who embrace the entitlement culture and those who cherish individual responsibility. In my opinion, Fluke is a moral and intellectual lightweight. For anyone to demand free stuff simply to support a lifestyle, and claim it a health issue, should make every sensible human being sick to their stomach. She is an emblem of a crumbling country, the strident entitlist (another word I coined; every time you use it, I get a royalty) who demands you tolerate her needs—while, of course, she ignores yours. We are now a nation of nags, each one crying out for something they feel is deserved rather than earned.

But the Fluke story took another turn—as it should, because it was starting to get boring—when radio talk show host Rush Limbaugh committed what sportsmen might call an "unforced error," veering into what the left calls "highly demeaning" territory, referring to Fluke as a "slut" and a "prostitute." The media and their lefty activists who supply them with fodder went ape-crazy, demanding apologies and firings and amputations. Sure, what Rush said was unnecessary, but it was only a parodic extension. A woman is demanding you pay for her sexual activities. Every single day must be covered. A left-wing comedian could come up with a half dozen monikers for that, and none of them very pretty. And he or she would get away with it. It's a joke, an exaggeration—one that didn't work in this case, though, because Fluke is a heroic character for the left, and the slur came from the mouth of Rush, the font of all things evil. Meanwhile, in various parts of the world, there are "slut" marches, led by feminists who want to proudly wear that moniker to strike a blow against an evil, intolerant patriarchy who would see sexually active women as immoral. For them, it's "empowering" to get laid a lot with casual aquaintances, which falls perfectly in line with millions of dudes who think it's pretty cool, too. No protest marches against that, I predict.

And so what could have been a frank discussion about government overreach and entitlement shifted into a "war on women." If you deny a birth control pill to anyone, period, you are waging war on the fairer sex. Ironically, the "I am woman, hear me roar" crowd became the "I am needy, give me more" bunch—the damsels in distress who, in 2012, cannot find a way to pay for cheap pills. I mean, aren't women independent enough not to need Daddy to take care of them?

And by Daddy, I mean President Obama, who actually called Fluke to offer his support. Yep, forget those protesters dying in Syria or the explosive number of homicides in Chicago. The person who needed his help most was a thirty-year-old woman whose mission is to get free stuff everyone can afford. The only missing part of this is that Obama did not personalize it and proudly proclaim, "When my daughters get old enough, I want them to get free contraception." Of course, he wouldn't, because he's a decent dad, and talking about your kids' future sex life would be legitimately weird. But that's where his logic leads, right? What's good for Fluke is good for all women.

But more important, Fluke did not need his help. In the age of the tolerati, the victim of a slur like "slut" never emerges as the victim but as the victor. Can you imagine *Newsweek* running an unhinged cover photo of Fluke, the way they did to Michele Bachmann? Not on your life. Rush calling Fluke those names (albeit jokingly and crudely), and President Obama calling her for comfort, are the greatest things to ever happen to Fluke. And likely will be, until her Guggenheim grant comes through.

If she doesn't get a job on MSNBC or Current TV by the time this here book is published, I will eat my hat. (Provided it's a small hat and made from a variety of marzipan. I love marzipan.) As I edit this book, she's about to take the podium at the 2012 DNC.

Having said that, I'm sure Fluke is a nice lady. I just have a quarrel with the entitlement mindset. And remember, she's only thirty. Maybe when she grows up, she'll get it.

THE BIGOT SPIGOT

I WAS BORN IN 1964—A GOOD YEAR for America (for that reason). But I remember none of it because back then I was too busy pooping and peeing in places I shouldn't. Not much has changed. But being born in that year made me a teen in the mid-seventies, where I witnessed the romanticization of the hilariously decadent decade that came before. I didn't remember the sixties, but I didn't have to—the entertainment industry and the media did it for me, creating a metastatic myth of the heroic protester, the Summer of Love dude who somehow became more majestic than men of similar age fighting in places where many never came back alive. The 1960s began the love affair with the outspoken liberal, the raging professor, the "one who would speak truth to power."

Were I naive enough, I would think that this noisy activity would be viewed as heroic, no matter the cause. If you were angry about the war—or abortion—it didn't matter as long as you made your voice heard, loud and clear. It didn't matter if that voice was shrill, clueless, self-indulgent. But I was wrong. It seems speaking truth to power is only tolerated if it's for the right causes, the right ideology. Sorry, by "right" I mean causes of the left. Yelling about the war—good. Yelling about unborn babies—bad.

Look, I know the media wants us to think the 1960s were

some kind of organic garden of natural protests, but I have my suspicions. My gut tells me the whole era has been exaggerated, like a shitty bachelor party in the eighties that now has become the stuff of legend. (There hasn't been a good bachelor party since . . . maybe ever.) And I know I'm right. There hadn't been a truly organic protest movement in decades, and then around 2009, we had one. And the media laughed.

It was a volatile period a few years back, when the health care bill was rammed through Congress like a torn-up dollar bill in a Coke machine. In response, a few angry people dared to question the modes and methods of this bizarre event. The bill was written to be enormously long, so in fact no one dared read it for fear of dying from exhaustion. Even Nancy Pelosi, the real commander in chief (at least domestically) at this point, and the bill's main promoter, confessed to not reading the monstrosity. Hell, she couldn't even lift it. The way the bill was forced through passage made Caligula's method of government seem positively modest—and he appointed a horse to the Senate. America sensed they'd just been snookered, and they were angrier than a wolverine with hemorrhoids.

And so all around the country, folks showed up at town hall meetings to question their representatives—and granted, it got pretty goofy. I hate it when people yell in public, especially when it's me and I've had too much to drink and not enough clothing on. And normal folks shaking with rage, unnerving congressmen with shouted questions and insults, looked unseemly and rude.

But I had to give them some credit. In this case, they were right. They got bamboozled. I also forgive them for their rawness. It was a first-time thing, for almost all of them. They were not seasoned pros like Bill Ayers, Van Jones, or Barack Obama. These were soccer moms, small-business owners, factory employees. You know, the 99 percent.

Now, you'd expect this sort of natural expression of outrage to be championed in the media. You'd expect reporters to look at these outbursts and draw teary-eyed comparisons to protests of the past, and announce in the paper of record that "the public is alive and well, and willing to confront government overreach."

Yeah, right. The media saw the whole thing as comical. Who were these funny old people, and where did they come from? Some of them look like stunt doubles from late-night Hoveround commercials.

It became clear that tolerance for speaking truth to power only exists if it's the power the media dislikes. Sure, you can laugh when an Iraqi throws a shoe at President Bush, but you'd better not call a Democratic congressman on the carpet. And worse, you'd better not question the imperatives of President Obama—the media's Jesus, whose religion, of course, is big government. It's the only religion the media seems to really fear (besides Islam).

Which is why, on some networks, you'd find a mocking smirk play on the faces of those reporting on the events. When these protests grew into Tea Party events, so did the media's disdain for them. Remember CNN's Susan Roesgen at a Chicago Tea Party back in 2009, accusing the crowd of hating her network, and interrupting the very people she came to interview? After getting nailed for it, CNN was forced to respond. A spokesperson named Christa Robinson said of Susan, "She was doing her job, and called it like she saw it."

Yeah, that's the problem. To quote Madge the manicurist describing how Palmolive softens your hands as you do the dishes, you don't notice the bias, because, "you're soaking in it."

Why were the media so hard on the Tea Parties and the folks at the town halls? Well, the media loves it when a story matches their assumptions perfectly. And that story always starts and ends with race.

Fact is, the moment you bothered to question Obama, simply by questioning the bill, you were a hater—of black presidents, old people, infants, and ferrets. The health care bill was supposed to be good for us, and we refused to see it because of our unconscious hatred for anything different.

Or black.

And so if you didn't support Obama's massive health care overhaul, you were pretty much rejecting peace, love, and understanding. The idea of tolerance only applies to those who blindly follow the new agenda. But even more vile, your right to critically ask questions became inextricably linked to an undercurrent of bigotry: you hate health care reform because Obama is black. After all, most of these protests were filled with older white folk—certainly they must hate a black man. By using repressive tolerance as a weapon, many in the media were effectively trying to silence those who simply were expressing themselves over a messy, horrible bill that even liberals like Nancy Pelosi admit they didn't read (can't say I blame her—hard to move those eyes when they're stuck in one position). These were the most benign protesters in the history of protesting, yet they were portrayed as an army of Archie Bunkers.

So if you want to see intolerance masked as tolerance, witness how the media treated the first real protest movement in years. If that uprising had been a liberal one, it would have garnered complete, slavish coverage, complete with tears, embedded reporters, and over-the-top documentaries. There would have been analogies to the sixties, profiles of the participants, celebrity visits, and journalistic defectors.

And it did. That uprising did take place a few years later, in the form of Occupy Wall Street. The media took to it like basmati on rice. Hilariously, the media identified with the protests, and were more than willing to pay them the respect they refused to afford the health care protesters or those folks at the Tea Party events. But because the Tea Partiers were not young leftists, not under or over grads, or completely ignorant of the entire Rage Against the Machine discography, they were mocked.

Probably the most insidious part of all this is that the Tea Partiers were new to the world of political agitprop. Unlike those who agitated for animal rights, or at the WTO protests, these folks worked for a living. Amazingly, the media chose to mock those who for the first time in their lives left their living rooms to carry a sign. Meanwhile, they backed the clichéd establishment protester, the career sign-carrier, the one who protests for anything or everything as long as its motto somehow denigrates America. You would think the media would have been more tolerant to the newbies, and would have grown tired of the sameness of the predictable hacks that came before. Not on your life.

It's why, to this day, in movies, you will never find an academic portrayed as a socialist propagandist. It's why in any TV series, you will never find a journalist portrayed as a left-wing hack with preconceived notions about the innate badness of our country. You will never ever see a conservative who isn't batshit crazy. You will never see a Christian who doesn't want to jail gays (or isn't secretly gay himself). Even though all of those examples are far more real than anything you'll find being pumped out of Hollywood, or what Andrew Breitbart accurately called "the complex."

This is because all of these examples—all representing a make-believe world where common sense reigns—cannot be tolerated. The town hall protesters and the Tea Partiers represented everything that the media had been ridiculing for the last forty years. They were their parents. These virgin protesters represented the media's narrow-minded stereotypes of idiot Americans previously fabricated in classrooms. The Tea Party was just another example of the racist, closed-minded asshole. Now he's off the recliner and in the street. And God and Abbie Hoffman help us—there are a lot of them. A flabby, gray army.

Compare that to how the media portrayed the union protesters in Wisconsin, where ghoulish signs and aggressive behavior were "tolerated," because they were up against those who hate the "working man." Never mind that those who were up against the unions were also "working men," who grossly outnumber the sliver of the population belonging to public unions. They were deemed offensive because they were taking food, health care, and paychecks from struggling teachers. Teachers who have the whole summer off. It's an intriguing contrast: As long as you're on the side of those deemed most tolerant, you can pretty much act any way you want. If only I had known this earlier, I would have fully embraced leftism and become a protester, and I'd probably be having sex right now in a tent with a girl named after a flower. Or a guy. I'm sure, at that point, it won't matter. I'll have already ingested the bath salts.

THE VAGINA DEMAGOGUES

HERE'S A JOKE: Why did the feminist cross the road? Because the pedestrian light turned green and opposing traffic had stopped, making the distance traveled perfectly safe. (By law, all feminist jokes cannot be funny.)

Anyway, as you probably already know, feminists demand apologies over insults to women they like, but drag their heels if the victim herself isn't part of the feminist brood. In a strange kind of mental contortionism, the concept of tolerance demands that you accept intolerant slander.

And this slander is spewing from people who, by proclaiming themselves feminists, get the FFP from the media. The Feminist Free Pass is the most insidious form of tolerance: as long as you toe the progressive line, you can be a FOP (a Full-On Pig). The most obvious offender was Bill Clinton, who proved that as long as you accept all the feminist tenets, you can treat women who aren't your wife as receptacles for your errant, undisciplined sperm. If you're a progressive, you can be the Johnny Appleseed of sexual conquest—from randy politicians like Teddy Kennedy, to celebrities who speak about women's rights while banging drugged-up teens in hot tubs (see Roman Polanski). But what I find most entertaining, of course, is how celebrities, talking heads, and assorted brainless activists can unload vicious vitriol on anyone who may not fall in line with their political assumptions—and get away with it.

Let us not forget America's favorite rapist, Mike Tyson, who on ESPN radio brought down the house one day with his cogent analysis of what it would be like to manhandle Sarah Palin.

We won't quote the maniac in full, because it's gross. On the program, the hosts nimbly brought up a rumor about Palin. The conversation turned toward the wholesome, as Tyson figured Palin needed a stronger lover. He's like a therapist! With a rape conviction!

My point: imagine, if you will, a conservative athlete had said the same thing about, say, Michelle Obama, or Nancy Pelosi, or Hillary Clinton. Everyone at ESPN would have been fired. Especially since most of them were guffawing like pimply-faced teens in homeroom. But we can forgive them, for their hearts are in the right place. They're libs. And so, instead, here in the primordial slime that spawned Keith Olbermann, they got a pass. Modern tolerance dictates that a liberal—even one that was convicted of rape like Tyson—gets away with this muck because his target is so reviled for being who she is. And who is she? Just a conservative chick who dared to challenge their anointed flag-bearer, Barack Obama.

Now, it's hard to find someone who's lower than Mike Tyson on the food chain. In fact, you'd have to venture into the animal world. I'd vote for maybe a mole, or perhaps some kind of hermaphroditic worm—so luckily there's Larry Flynt. If Larry were a conservative, it would be perfectly acceptable to make light of his paralysis—he was shot, and now gets around town sunk in an expensive electric wheelchair. But since the man—famous for a cover featuring a nude woman dropped in a blender—is for women's rights (I'm fairly certain that boils down to letting chicks degrade themselves in *Hustler*), he's now a folk hero with an Oscar-nominated movie about him. The great thing about tolerance: You can create the most vile pornography on the planet, and Hollywood will fall at your feet—in the name of . . . tolerance! Hence, he can get away with saying this about Palin and her disabled child:

> [Palin] did a disservice to every woman in America. She knew from the first month of pregnancy that kid was going to be Down's syndrome. It's brain-dead. A virtual vegetable. She carries it to all these different political events against abortion; she did it just because she didn't want to say she'd had an abortion. How long is it going to live? Another twelve, fifteen years? Doesn't even know it's in this world. So what kind of compassionate conservative is she? I don't think anybody will want her near the White House.

You have to admit, it's staggering seeing a vegetable calling someone else a vegetable. If Larry Flynt had come across Larry Flynt after the shooting, he would have smothered him with a pillow. So why does a legendary pervert who once had sex with a chicken (it's in his memoir) see fit to say such things? *Because he can.* A champion of FFP and a victim of LBSS (or Liberal Blind Spot Syndrome), he has lost all context of what's considered appropriate language about women or children. I suppose if I said I'd love to wheel him off a cliff because his life is not worth living, I'd have to retract that statement and apologize quickly. So I won't.

We've gotten to a place where a well-respected columnist can fabricate the most elaborate fantasies about Sarah Palin, because, well, he can. While we ridicule (and by "we" I mean myself and my slew of honeygliders that live in a cage under my bed) the birther conspiracies about President Obama or 9/11 truthers, the same cannot be said for the insanity spewing from Daily Beast columnist Andrew Sullivan's addled brain. He was once a promising writer but he got comfortable. After surrounding himself with Palin-haters, he threw his hairy body full force into the craziest of theories—the kind that would get you institutionalized if you didn't have a famous byline. To recap, here is Sullivan's take on her baby Trig:

> The medical term for Down syndrome is Trisomy-21 or Trisomy-g. It is often shortened in medical slang to Tri-g. Is it not perfectly possible that the very name given to this poor child, being reared by Bristol, is another form of mockery of his condition, along with the retarded baby tag? And does the way in which this poor child was hauled around the country on a book tour, being dragged out in front of flash photographs in the middle of the night, barely clothed, suggest someone who actually cares for children with special needs, or rather sees them as a way to keep the spotlight on her?

Um, so wait. It's not just *you* mocking the child, it's actually the parents! Well, that gets you off the hook, uh, I guess. Worse than this quivering analysis (almost joyous in its brutality) is that it's excusable by the usually sensitive left. You can tolerate everything I suppose, including not tolerating a mom who decides to give birth and raise a child with challenges. Don't you think this is slightly weird coming from a gay man? I mean, given the fact that homosexuals were some of the first to be exterminated in any attempt at a "pure race," you'd think he'd support Palin for sticking to her own beliefs about all life being sacred. Guess not, especially if all your tolerant friends just find the whole damn thing perfectly hysterical. And by "friends," I mean the Greek chorus of liberal blog-readers who echo your every synaptic spasm when they should be doing their freshman English home-work. I've only met Sullivan once, but I'm kinda certain he's off his rocker, although I'm sure he'd tell you he's damned if he's not tolerant. And Obama describes his analysis as brilliant.

Which brings me to Keith Olbermann, the most tolerant man in the universe, provided you agree with his own intolerant idi-ocy. There may be no man on the planet more filled with joyous adolescent hate for women. The things he's said about Michelle Malkin (a lipsticked pig, as he so fondly called her) alone qualify him for the Douchebag Hall of Fame.

But for some odd reason he focused on a not-so-famous writer who's appeared on my show countless times, S. E. Cupp. Here's what he had to say about Ms. Cupp, a truly awful, reprehensible, doesn't-deserve-to-live person (I kid the Cupp—she wears really cute glasses).

> On so many levels [S. E. Cupp's] a perfect demonstration of the necessity of the work Planned Parenthood does.

"On so many levels"? What a delightful way of denigrating women! Essentially, it boils down to this: I hate the fact that you're a con-servative female so much that you should have been aborted! So where does this vitriol come from, in Olby's case?

It's pretty simple: Cupp is a very smart and very capable person who would never sleep with something as grotesque as Olbermann. If you asked Cupp, my guess is she'd rather sleep with a mummified sea urchin. And who can blame her? This could explain why Olby is almost always alone, looking lost, sad, and angry. But did he get any grief for what he said? Not at all, because he picked on a conservative woman. And they are fair game. See, if you're pro-life, then clearly you're already against women, so even pigs like Keith can say vicious things about you. You don't tolerate abortion as birth control, therefore you shall not be tolerated—or viewed as a human being.

At a certain point you'd think this kind of crap would get old. But in the world of tolerance, intolerance flourishes, for acceptance of different points of view is wholly unacceptable. God bless them for their monumental hypocrisy. I only hope Keith finally does have offspring and it eats him.

Sounds over-the-top? I don't know. One thing I've learned about tolerance is that you can't tolerate a fetus. They're just so damn annoying. They just lie there and make your life difficult. A fetus takes up room in your body, puts off your career, and all in all is a drain on your finances. They keep you home from protests. They keep you from running off to Catalina with your cute philosophy professor (he's so tortured). And worst of all, unless you're a Hollywood celebrity who can pay for round-the-clock nannies, they make you grow the fuck up. Frankly, how fetuses convinced us to let them into our exclusive club called society is beyond me. It is the best club in the world, and needs someone stronger working the door. I have an idea: why not Democrat Gwen Moore?

Here's what she had to say about unborn kids.

> I just want to tell you a little bit about what it's like to not have Planned Parenthood. You have to add water to the formula to make it stretch. You have to give your kids ramen noodles at the end of the month to fill up their little bellies so they won't cry.

So true. These selfish little piles of protoplasm—if they are allowed to grow, they need to be watered, and that water is expensive. Filling up bellies is both time-consuming and a strain on your wallet, especially if you like to go clubbing. Buy a new smartphone. What Gwen is talking about reminds me of the philosophy of Casey Anthony: you can't let a baby get in the way of a girls' night out.

If anything, the real victims of repressive tolerance are the unborn. In the name of choice—or rather, tolerating the choice—we cannot tolerate that inconvenience. When feminists see what Palin did, to them, it reminds them that there is a universal tolerance that dwarfs their own narrow definition. It makes them feel small and selfish.

And extermination is always the go-to place for the tolerant when they find someone they cannot tolerate. Remember Chris Titus? Of course you don't. He was a comedian who had a short-lived TV show, based on his own troubled life. It was god-awful, but we tolerated it anyway, because it came from a place of pain. Yeah, we had to tolerate his bad jokes and self-absorbed meanderings because he "hurt" inside. But knowing pain doesn't mean he cannot inflict it on others. When faced with the idea of a Palin presidency, Titus said:

> You know what, man? I am going to literally—if [Palin] gets elected president, I am going to hang out on the grassy knoll all the time, just loaded and ready—because you know what? It's for

my country. It's for my country. If I got to sacrifice myself, it's for my country.

What country is he talking about, exactly? The United States of Paranoid Has-Beens? Well, it's a country shaped, in his mind, by LBSS. With Liberal Blind Spot Syndrome, it's perfectly okay to say you're going to kill Palin, because in the tolerant worldview, she's exempt. Consider the crimes she's committed: she's pro-life, she's from Alaska, and she doesn't adhere to the typical mindset you find among the pathetic comic groupies that Titus plies his wares on when he's sulking through various shitholes he's been forced to perform in. She is not one of them, so he can imagine her killed. He did this schtick on *The Adam Carolla Show.* I love Carolla, and I get his gig: he lets comedians talk and doesn't correct their idiocy. Or maybe that level of idiocy was just too much to correct in one show.

Titus knew the score, and knew it could help his "career." Somewhat. Later he had to explain himself, which he did poorly— offering a quasi-apology, then justifying his words pathetically. I'd repeat them here, but really, there's almost nothing worse than making an apology when you don't believe in it and you don't have to. He could have just said, "Yeah, I hate Palin. So what?" But he didn't. Catch him soon, at a strip mall near you. He'll be performing there nightly. If you call washing dishes at Sbarro and hitting on teenage goths at Hot Topic "performing."

A PEP SMEAR

THE NETWORK WHERE I work is evil, or so I am told by people who don't watch it. Which is why my employer is the only media enterprise exempt from the warm hug of tolerance. A half dozen media groups are devoted to tripping it up. Endless comedians, bloggers, and talking heads devote most of their mental energies to demonizing the network. And why? Because out of a media culture that is purely liberal—from newspapers, to networks, to music and entertainment—one entity rejects such easy assumptions about the world. And for the modern, tolerant liberal, that simply cannot be tolerated. Everyone must be in lockstep—before we can disagree, apparently.

Now, this chapter is not meant to be a whine on media but a gentle salute to those people who endure the slings and arrows of the oh-so-tolerant, who somehow feel threatened by a group of people who question their long-held, lazy opinions. And it's also a less than gentle rebuke to those who can't handle an alternative news source being around at all.

Shouldn't the tolerant, so confident in their beliefs, not worry about disagreement? Shouldn't they actually embrace it? They don't. They won't. And they make my job a lot of fun because of it. And certainly a lot easier.

But the tolerance troops do not just express themselves through hectoring, weepy lectures. They can also sneak up on you under the guise of reasonable jocularity. "Come on, man" is one way of putting this mode of persuasion. Or more precisely, "Come on, man, you really don't believe that." You often hear this from an easygoing liberal when you say, "Without the media, Obama would have been creamed in the election." Or when you claim, "The constant global warming threat is exaggerated." The "Come on, man, you don't believe that" is their way of saying, "You're too sane to actually believe that. Don't you want to be one of us? Cool people don't say what you say. After all, you live on one of the coasts. You're in media. You're not Amish. You can't really believe that!"

Anything political that I ever say on TV is greeted by my liberal friends with this kind of friendly but exasperated response. They're like a fancy waiter who can't believe you requested ketchup.

This kind of lazy answer is a great way for the tolerant to terminate debate—because in your heart you want to be liked by your friends and peers, and they're promising you that gift if you just stop raising questions about their cemented liberal dogma. Liberalism is the one-way ticket to backslapping approval among the cool kids, which makes it about as rebellious as a divorced dad getting an earring from the local mall's Piercing Pagoda.

The best purveyor of this cheery semi-intolerance is the talented and funny Jon Stewart. His show is a thirty-minute stretch on the one phrase "You can't be serious." His targets are almost always on the right (and granted, a lot of those targets make it *really* easy for him), rarely on the left. And when he does hit someone on the left, you almost have to feel grateful for it. He's been doing it more often, God bless him.

To understand this kind of soft condemnation of the right,

let's turn to Stewart's Rally to Protect Liberalism. It wasn't actually called that, but it should have been, simply for the sake of honesty. Just a few days before the 2010 midterm elections, Stewart and Stephen Colbert held the Rally to Restore Sanity—an event masquerading as an inclusive, fun rejection of all things crazy. I'm sure that having it right before the midterms (in which the Dems were about to be slaughtered) was just some bizarre coincidence!

Anyway, they called it a Million Moderate March—*moderate* being the apt word for an appropriate, hipster response to anyone who might be pissed off about health care reform, President Obama, Nancy Pelosi, or anything else that all the cool kids were okay with. It's also a slap in the head to anyone who isn't cool—and it played off the massively popular (and, according to the media, sinister) Glenn Beck rallies, which, despite the revival-like flair, were actually disarmingly calm and picnicky but still posed a threat to earnest libs, who own the right to protest. Still, the fact that first-timers were organizing made these goofy white Christians in their khakis ripe for ridicule by an acerbic, charming, media-savvy Manhattan millionaire. The longer I live, the more I'm convinced the world is just one big high school, with the cool kids always targeting the uncool.

So instead of being an innocent celebration of "Lighten up, dude—we're all friends here just having fun," it appeared, at least to me, to be a stunt meant to undermine the resurgent right. It's exactly the thing that that bald, nerdy guy in glasses from the *New York Times* subscription commercial might attend and feel totally good about himself for days afterward, while lounging on a blanket in Central Park with a round of runny cheese and a bottle of light Sancerre. It's something that attracted celebrities who want to appear politically astute without rubbing too many people the wrong way. It was for ideological wusses, who liked dipping their toes in the pool without getting wet.

Which raises an interesting question: Would Stewart have announced his event if those Tea Party events had had a decidedly liberal tilt?

Short answer: No.

Long answer: Noooooooooooo.

The evidence for this is pretty simple: there would have been no rally at all, if the Dems were doing great. There would have been no rally if no one raised a hackle (whatever that is) about health care reform. Stewart was responding to hostility to the Obama administration. The anger, to Stewart, seemed disproportionate to the actual cause. And he could be right—except that he's never done it before.

Which makes the joke wear thin, at least to me. Think about it: What Stewart is doing is not speaking truth to power but poking fun at the people who are speaking truth to power. I mean, Stewart isn't going after politicians, he's mocking people who are. While the Tea Party is a bottom-up phenomenon, Stewart is actually on the very, very top looking down. His rally was a reaction from the establishment, not against it. He's saying, "Come on, man—we got a cool president. You people are raging dorks. Why are you rocking the boat? You're not the ones who get to do that—we are! You aren't the ones we were waiting for!"

Here's more proof: Leading up to Stewart's event, Democrats actually complained that the rally might hurt their chances in the midterm elections. They worried that their supporters would be more inclined to focus on the rally before the election rather than campaign or vote. The rally would, in effect, replace the election in that feel-good exercise called "doing your part." It would be like eating dessert before dinner.

And maybe the Dems were right. They got trounced. But I'm pretty sure those results had to do more with anger toward the administration and less with Stewart's goofing around with his celebrity pals on the political stage. In the end: no one cared. A bunch of libs got to have their "cool kid" status confirmed, Stewart boosted his ratings for a few days, and Colbert trotted out his talking-like-a-republican-is-a-parody-in-itself schtick. I guess to some it never gets old. And even I admit it makes me giggle.

But this is what passes for rebellion in media, which is really just making fun of people in fanny packs who prefer Sarah Palin over Sarah Silverman. That's the line that's drawn, and it's one I cross all the time. I think Palin is delightfully quirky and Silverman viciously funny. I also sympathize with Palin's constant humiliations by the tolerant cool set (I can't think of a single public figure other than Palin whose disabled child is such a gleeful object of derision), and see Silverman resort too many times to lazy PC humor in order to get a drive-by laugh from a pliant audience. I find both women invigorating, but it's clear one is more a victim of intolerance than the other. And someone needs to tell Silverman that her fascination with her bodily functions isn't mirrored in the public at large (exception: the fat dude at tech support. I wish he'd stop telling me about it).

So that rally was not for me. The bottom line of its existence: "We're cool, they're crazy." In other words, we pretend to be tolerant, but everyone who disagrees with us is a crazy racist in a tricorn hat. The true irony: In an event where the goal was to celebrate getting along and peachy-keen tolerance, they invited Yusuf Islam, previously known as Cat Stevens, to sing. A beacon of intolerance, he encouraged the assassination of Salman Rushdie over his tome *The Satanic Verses,* which he found to be critical of Islam. He is about as peaceful as the guy who hangs out on the corner of my street shouting at lampposts. But he's been around long enough, and he used to be Cat Stevens so he's cool. He's one of them! A violent extremist—but fun nonetheless! He plays acoustic guitar! How cool is it to have the guy who sang that song you used to make out to in the dorms back in the eighties! And how lucky we are to have prolonged our college years indefinitely!

The media, however, was having too good a time with the whole circus to really give a damn about that, because that circus was one that they wanted to be part of. And I'm including even a few of my friends who attended the rally. (And by "friends," I mean people I now plan on mailing unsolicited magazine subscriptions to.) According to them, it was good, clean, hip fun. People were friendly, the mood was upbeat, the girls were pretty. The event was a huge success. And a 100,000-strong circle jerk.

Which, because that takes stamina, reminded me of my past at Rodale—a health publishing company. While I was an editor there, I was one of a handful of conservatives, out of a company of thirteen hundred people. The folks there were mostly young, cool, and sinewy—just like the others I worked with while running *Stuff* and *Maxim UK* (but without the cocaine). Some were "make our voices heard" types, or "awareness raisers," or "rally attendees."

My point: Every single day of my life was a Jon Stewart rally. I knew Jon Stewart, figuratively—before the world did. Everyone around me was pleasant, usually white, and always reveling in their reflexive assumptions about the "rest" of less hip America. Which translates, of course, as most of America, particularly between the coasts. Yep, they were my people when we drank and did assorted narcotics in various Midtown dive bathrooms. But when they would find out who I would be voting for (usually by asking me, and then staring at me in disbelief), they'd give me the "You can't be serious. Come on, man." And when I didn't respond the way they wanted, they'd turn into Jon Stewarts en masse.

That's why, when I watched Stewart's rally, I just thought, "Same old same old." Who needs it? I also finally discovered where all those people I stopped hiring for freelance work ended up.

There was a real divide between two groups: The Tea Party was about candidates; the sanity rally was about celebrity. More important, the Tea Party was a civilian reaction to our government's sprint toward progressivism. The rally, however, was a celebrity reaction to those civilians.

The rally boiled down to a comical intolerance of people who just aren't cool. The Tea Party! I mean, these people bowl—unironically! It was all just too Marie Antoinette for me—rich, smug celebrities and their Coldplay-loving acolytes giving a collective smirk to their hapless parents, who just never got with the program. *Mom, Dad . . . what are we going to do with you?*

So the real title of the event shouldn't have been The Rally to Restore Sanity but The Rally to Ignore Insanity. Because that was the message. The Tea Partiers are reacting to alarming stuff: the insane spending, the bottomless deficit, weird appointments of people like Van Jones (with a deep antipathy toward Western values), political arrogance—it's real anxiety over real trouble for future offspring. True, the problem started way before Obama, but did it get any better? We've got trillions more in debt, and a brand-new entitlement bill engineered by Nancy Pelosi that no one bothered to read. And those who were ringing the alarm were just average citizens.

Stewart's rally says, "Ignore that. Check out Cat Stevens!" With a load of flashy entertainment and edgy personalities—they're the band playing on the *Titanic,* enjoying the applause while we approach the iceberg (i.e., Greece, or an actual iceberg).

Of course, maybe I'm just biased. Back in June 2011, Jon Stewart debated a news anchor at my place of employment over media bias. He stated that doing *The Daily Show* is harder than what my coworkers do. But, sorry, in my opinion, the first and only preparation *The Daily Show* does is making jokes about people the writers disagree with. Though I didn't do a survey, I can bet that all of his writers are liberal—so all you're going to get are jokes targeted at people they find ridiculous. Conservatives. The uncool.

Stewart—in his tussles with various anchors at the nework—made a big issue about them laying off President Bush while going after Obama—which, as I've said before in other places, is nuttier than squirrel poop. Let's not forget that while Bush was president, he was trashed by a left-wing posse who delighted in military defeat, for it meant their side was winning. To them, dissent was patriotic even if it meant dead troops. As many have pointed out, if the casualties during World War Two were reported the same way they were during Iraq, we'd all be speaking Belgian. (We fought Belgium, right? Or was it Mexico? I majored in English Lit.)

My network wasn't ignoring Bush's actions. Maybe it was reacting to what I would call Patriotic Terrorism. I saw a fully realized, anti-America lynch mob who would rather win an election than a war, and that made me more of a righty than 9/11, my life at Berkeley, and all my head injuries combined.

Want to see proof of my point? Ask yourself where is this fe-verish antiwar movement now that Obama got into power. Obama has killed more terrorists than anyone in recent memory (God bless him for that), and you don't hear much of a peep from any-one other than Michael Moore (who even Karl Marx would have termed a commie pinko). Gitmo is still open, doing more business than your local Hampton Inn, but that ceases to be an issue now that their guy is in office. Remember, Gitmo was the albatross around Bush's neck—now it's the puka shells around Obama's neck (a shout-out to his tiny island nation, Hawaii). As of this writing, we're still losing troops in Afghanistan, for purposes ever more attenuated from our original mission there. Where's the out-rage? The "not in our name" marches? The judging on *Dancing with the Stars* gets more scrutiny.

On one of my shows, a cohost took issue with my accusation that Stewart was smarmy. He said, "Smarmy is one word. I'd say brave. He came into the lion's den and defended himself."

Which isn't surprising. My cohost, whom I love like a de-mented little brother, is like everyone I worked with in media—someone who considers himself apolitical, until he runs into someone like me, who isn't a liberal. Apolitical, in the media, means decidedly liberal and not used to being challenged. So I get that he sees Stewart as brave. But this is no lion's den—because the lion's den is the world that contains my network. Think about it: A few years back, the *New York Times* ran a piece pointing out the dearth of conservatives in journalism, theater, therapy, and academia. Which, considering the collective out-put of those fields, I would take as a resounding compliment. You've had, for a long spell, a Democratic House, a Democratic Senate, a Democrat for president, a liberal media, a left-wing

Hollywood, a liberal arts and music culture. You've got it all, and you're mad because one entity isn't playing ball? What happened to that whole "Dissent is patriotic" thing? It seems we only look right because everything else is left. Stewart (and my cohost) are both blissfully unaware of their own biases because, cue Madge, they're soaking in it. Stewart coming into the "lion's den" of an atypical network was about as "brave" as the Soviet Union invading Hungary. And no matter how hard a time Stewart may have gotten there, he knew 95 percent of the media had his back. His "schooling" of those guys was heroic. I'll bet the columns lauding Stewart's rally were written the night before it happened.

And more amazingly, even with the deck so stacked in their favor, the left still can't seal the deal. Because their message just doesn't jibe with the American public, whose center-right stances are revealed in poll after poll. Talk about snatching defeat from the jaws of victory—this is a collapse of Red Soxian magnitude.

A perfect example of the mythical tolerant media type can be found in the JournoList scandal—a blip in the battle of media bias that you probably never heard of (nor had to hear of, if you, unlike me, have a life). The JournoList scandal was a microcosm of the media's inherent bias. Imagine if a group of conservative reporters conspired to undermine their political adversaries by making up rumors that they're racist scum. Once unmasked, they would be condemned to unemployment. However, JournoList was a group of liberal writers and bloggers who did that exact thing. In short, it was a group of insider-y writers and bloggers who belonged to an online salon—something dorks do to feel less dorky. But within this goofy cabal, members were secretly encouraging one another to call out anyone they disagreed with as intolerant, as a bigot, as a racist. Once exposed by other bloggers, they disbanded—but not without a strong defense made by friends in the media. Fact is, here you had a tolerant group of people preaching intolerance against those who disagree with them—and actually encouraging a particularly vile dishonesty to achieve their ideological objectives.

And can you just picture them meeting to plan this thing? How palpable do you suppose the "dangerous lefty cell" pretensions were? I bet they were smoking their allotted four cigarettes a year, wearing berets. I can almost hear the zither music.

But the bigger issue . . . was that it wasn't seen as a big issue. Come on, they're the cool kids, just going after the uncool kids! If you disagree with them, you probably are a loathsome bigot, so even if you've never said a racist thing in your life, you're thinking of it anyway. We can tell. But the fact is, if you're so confident in your beliefs, then this idea of creating a secret society of journalists to go after your enemies would be unnecessary. Apparently, McCarthyism is entirely acceptable, if you're cool.

This thinking can be found elsewhere, primarily with the left-wing outfit Media Matters, which, in memos, has expressed a desire to pry into the personal lives of conservatives in media, simply because we don't share their assumptions. This should have been a bigger deal than it was, but it wasn't because everyone in the media feels the same way. If Media Matters had targeted a Brooklyn food co-op, it would be another matter. The fact is, MSNBC relies on Media Matters so heavily, as do other liberal writers at various major networks, that it allows this modern McCarthyism to exist. And I'm not referring to Joe McCarthy. I'm referring to the dummy—Charlie McCarthy. For Media Matters is the ventriloquist Edgar Bergen, and the liberal media is the dummy, moving its lips while the noise is supplied by the most progressive outfit since the Nehru jacket. At least Charlie was more of an independent thinker (something that I don't think Edgar ever got used to—tragic how that ended).

BUTCH CASSIDY AND
THE SUBSIDIZED KID

PER SQUARE FOOT, Hollywood has more tools than Ace Hardware. And because of this, disdain is often directed at people who deserve their gratitude. This behavior is most prevalent among celebrities and assorted artists, who express dismissive opinions toward supposedly simple or idiotic Americans. It's often done when traveling in other countries, Gwyneth Paltrow–style, even though it's directed at the home country that keeps them in Range Rovers made entirely of Fabergé eggs. And will someone at least break the news to "Gwinnie" that she's not British landed gentry? There hasn't been a more ridiculous Anglophile pose since Dick Van Dyke in *Chitty Chitty Bang Bang*. What a doofus.

In January, during all the hoopla (or as much hoopla as you could expect) leading up to the 2012 Sundance Film Festival, its founder, Robert Redford, went on a clumsy, brittle tirade against America, comparing it unfavorably to Europe—a favorite hobby among both the forgotten aging stars and the eager up-and-comers. Somewhere in Hollywood, there must be a *Celebrity Thoughts for Dummies* book, and the first chapter simply states "Compare America unfavorably to Europe." The second chapter: "Trash Palin." The third chapter: "Confess your third nipple."

While ripping on Republican Mitt Romney (suggesting Mitt would prefer a movie like *Transformers* over the arty crud at Sundance, essentially using Mitt as a symbol for "the rest of America"), Redford complained, incoherently, about how the U.S. lagged in appreciating the true artists and their artistry. The bloomin-onion-faced actor, recalling time spent as a student in Europe as a springboard to his current outlook, says, "For years and years and years, you've all experienced what we had to live with, the fact that other countries are far more supportive of their artists than we are." He adds, "But when you have congressional narrow-minded people, people who are afraid of change when change is the only thing that succeeds, the only thing we know is going to happen is that things are going to change. . . . I think it's just tragic that we don't support our artists more than we do. And as long as we're going to have that kind of thinking in Congress, we're going to have to fight it." I've cracked open fortune cookies with deeper thinking than this. And anyone who thinks a guy who like Redford spent his early "European years" doing anything more than drinking wine and bending costars over the radiator knows nothing about young men.

Translation of Redford's rant: I want to make crappy movies that nobody wants to see, and I want to pay for it with your tax dollars. Rather than make a movie that Americans might find entertaining, I want the government to go through your wallet while you're watching something good, like *Spaceballs*.

And while some Yanks might yearn to feel sophisticated and pseudo-intellectual and therefore agree with R^2, the truth is, if we instituted a referendum on a proposed "independent film tax" tomorrow, how far would it get, really?

And what if you did the same in Europe? You think the Italians would vote for such a thing? Only if the Germans were paying for it. And here's the other elephant in the room: Europe has "supported its artists" all the way to the brink of continental insolvency. They got change all right. Loose change. Which is the average GDP these days. "Yes, we're broke, but at least we've got mimes!"

But there's something else going on here. I do think a great movie can be an artistic experience (I am referring mainly to *Human Centipede* and *Human Centipede 2*), but generally movies are commerce. Films these days are just one step above your average video game, which means Redford is just another joystick with an agent at William Morris. He's not even a great artist. He's no Picasso, or Ernest Hemingway, or even Stephen King. Hell, he's not even Bruce Vilanch. He's a professional show-off who will likely be replaced by a hologram in a few years. In fact, judging from his recent "work," that may already have happened. That's the problem with most of Hollywood—talent supplanted by ego, and too much time in between actual jobs for that recipe to boil. I mean, c'mon. Artist? Really? For Hollywood actors? The guy who writes the obituaries for whatever paper you read is more of an artist than these professional behaviorists. I just don't buy it, sailor. They're indulged pubescents who never grew out of "let's put on a show for Mommy and Daddy." Somewhere along the line we let them start believing they were a big deal. They're not. Period.

And you gotta admit it's pretty convenient for Redford, after making dozens of big-studio flicks, to have made enough money to buy a city and then decided it's all about independent film. If we asked him if he'd like to go back and do it all over, and instead of the career he managed without help he had received a small government stipend to make documentaries about teachers who use Aztec macramé to reach at-risk felons, what do you think he'd choose? He'd be back on the studio lot whistling the theme to *The Sting* before you could say *The Way We Were.*

Of course, he could leave us unsophisticated American dopes and actually *move* to the more cosmopolitan Europe, where he'd never have to say, "I don't want to get into politics" and then get into politics, like we're not supposed to notice (see George Clooney). He'd never have to tolerate supremely American people (i.e., dull people with dull tastes) like Mitt Romney again, or great unwashed rubes who think Sundance is an Indian casino. But that would mean a much smaller stage, less acclaim, fewer ego strokes, and less money for periodic mole removal.

The problem with the intolerant artist is that he fails to see that we tolerate him—even more, we support him by buying his crap once in a while. That's the basic contract. And thinking Americans understand that government support for performance artists shoving yams up their ass doesn't bring national security, or a healthy economy, or even successful art. It brings Greece, where the movie theaters are empty because no one can afford to buy tickets. It also brings filthy yams, which can lead to a rare infection and a worm that later becomes your best friend. Mine's got his own blog at the Huffington Post.

A *REALLY* BAD DAY AT THE OFFICE

WE LIVE IN A TIME when our leaders seem hell-bent on legislating reality. The need to be seen as open-minded—coupled with a fear of being seen as racist—has culminated in an administration that struggles with calling a terrorist a terrorist. Driven by a desire to be viewed as NLB (Not Like Bush), Obama's administration has turned our basic lexicon into a game show of code words and charades. Whether it's the Fort Hood shooter or the underwear bomber, the preferred wisdom is that these are just incompetent crazies, not terrorists. Clowns, not killers. Bozos, not bad men.

This logic is so pervasive and poisonous it even infected Obama's onetime State Department spokesman P. J. Crowley, who couldn't bring himself to label the killings of American servicemen in Frankfurt by a lone jihadist an act of terror. Instead, he hypothetically—and pathetically—wondered if the Tucson tragedy (the shootings that brutally wounded Congresswoman Gabby Giffords and killed a handful of other innocent people) was an act of terror, too. It's the worst kind of moral relativism, born out of extreme wussiness.

How does this help fight terror, you ask? It doesn't—and thanks for asking, whoever you are.

Instead, it encourages a head-in-the-sand mentality that cedes extremists the moral high ground. And so this is why you have eight-year-old kids and eighty-year-old grannies getting felt up in airport security—because you can't frisk the Middle Eastern guy without performing the same task on others. Or else you'd be seen as profiling, which is racist, which is offensive, which is awful. So rather than focus on safety, we spread the diligent work out to a paper-thin veneer, making it that much easier to penetrate.

Probably the weirdest display of this bizarre over-the-top tolerance driven hysteria comes from a letter written by the Defense Department, in which they apparently classified the Fort Hood massacre as workplace violence. Yep, a horrible event, in which a rabid Islamist opened fire and killed American troops was labeled "workplace violence." Folks, I know workplace violence. In all its permutations. Trust me, Fort Hood isn't it. Thankfully, during a joint session of the Senate and House Homeland Security Committees, someone possessed enough sanity to call BS on it.

Senator Susan Collins blasted the department, and suggested political correctness was being put ahead of our national security. She then accurately nailed the Obama administration for being too timid in identifying radical Islam as the culprit.

She's right. I mean, when a guy shouts "Allahu akbar" while shooting more than a dozen troops, it's safe to say he isn't a Jehovah's Witness. He also isn't a disgruntled worker pissed off at his boss. Or annoyed that the vending machine is out of Snickers.

Another hero here: Senator Joe Lieberman, who held hearings on this stuff. Lieberman and his committee essentially broke ranks with the insanity of the Obama administration and labeled Major Hasan's actions not only terrorism but preventable terrorism that wasn't stopped because of political correctness in both the military and the FBI. Of course, Lieberman had to fight every inch of the way to get the necessary documents from Eric Holder's Justice Department. (See *Furious, Fast and.*) But we've all gotten to know Holder since then—we know what he's about. Imagine if Hasan had been a Southern white boy looking to shoot minorities or women. You think it would have been labeled "workplace violence"? You think it would have taken congressional hearings to find out why a guy like Hasan was allowed to do what he did, despite the investigations into him going on at the time? Forget it. Obama's DOJ wouldn't have even bothered with a trial. Al Sharpton would have declared the perp guilty. His secretary, Eric Holder, would concur. And Soledad O'Brien would indict America in a seven-part CNN special.

I mean, what would it take at that point to qualify as terror? My understanding of a terrorist is someone who invokes terror in others. Hasan didn't qualify for that as he was spraying Fort Hood with military grade ammo? I suspect there are a few people who were there who disagree.

This mentality also explains the government videos you can find online offering suggestions to the public on what they should do if they ever witness activity that might be terror-related. In these slick videos, you'd be hard-pressed to find anyone who looks, well, Arabic. Everyone looks European, or kinda European, and most look young, hip, and healthy. With the sound off, it could have been a commercial for your local community college. No, scratch that. The local college would actually include every single type from the diversity wish list—in effect *all* commercials are pretty much Benetton ads. Except the terror PSAs, which are entirely European, and therefore hideously bigoted. The PSAs have about as much color as my urine after drinking a case of Coors Light.

Now, when I first saw these ads, I experienced some mild discomfort. Not because the commercials seem to say Americans of European ancestry are more likely to blow us up than radical Islamics. No, I wondered about the poor actors of dark complexion who are being cheated out of jobs because, well, they're just too perfect for the part. We now live in a world where Corey Feldman has a better shot playing a terrorist than an actual terrorist. (No complaining there. Mr. Feldman is a dynamite actor with gentle, caring hands.) Yep, in an effort to be as tolerant as possible, we took jobs away from people who could use the money.

Where does this all come from? It's a disease that I was the first to name: Islamophobia-phobia. The fear of being accused of Islamophobia.

Islamophobic, by definition, seems to be a fear of Islam. But it's come to mean any behavior that's perceived as mean-spirited toward people who practice Islam. And by any behavior, I mean just about everything you do in life. Look, if you feel uncomfortable that a cabdriver named Mohammed Mohammed is talking incessantly on his Bluetooth, is that Islamophobic? Maybe. But the fact that you listen—that you clue into it—doesn't make you a racist. It makes you human.

And the accusation of Islamophobia prevents questions being asked that are far more important than that stupid one about the Bluetooth. And Islamophobia-phobia has now become a tool in hampering our war on terror and enabling our enemy to get away with more crap—by making us timid in our quest for safety.

Here are some facts that should make your head explode, whether you heard them already or not: Thirteen people were killed and dozens more wounded at Fort Hood. The killer, Major Nidal Hasan, did not hide his sympathies for radical Islam, for he was a radical himself, inspired by the now dead radical U.S. cleric Anwar al-Awlaki. The two lunatic loverboys even exchanged something like twenty e-mails (sometimes I imagine them as "God is great! Death to the infidels LOL"). If people had known about this crap (and it seems they did), and didn't act for fear of being seen as intolerant, then those thirteen poor souls perished because of pure moral cowardice. Along the way, some asshat felt it was far better to be seen as tolerant toward radical Muslims than to protect our own brave gals and guys. This is one of the more gruesome consequences of tolerance: you'd risk the lives of others in order to belong in the cool group. And because you are seen as tolerant (and therefore enlightened and cool), we have thirteen dead Americans.

It's no secret that since 9/11 the number of plots targeting our soldiers has gone up dramatically. There are something like thirty-three plots (according to a summary of incidents on FoxNews.com) that have been uncovered, and God knows how many others we don't even know about.

In June 2011, two men allegedly plotted to attack a military base near Seattle. Then, a month later, an Army private named Naser Abdo (probably Irish Catholic) was accused of planning a second attack on Fort Hood. And then there was Jose Pimentel, another Muslim, who in November 2011 was arrested because he allegedly planned to kill service members returning from war. And God, I hope he's off his rocker, but Congressman Peter King reports, there's evidence that a large number of extremists have—like Hasan—joined the armed services.

Now, somehow I just don't think viewing these threats as potential examples of workplace violence is going to be our most effective method of attack. What are we going to see on the walls next to the "no smoking" signs? Posters that exclaim, "No massacres in the name of Allah"?

Fact is, we are living under a government that's head over heels in love with euphemisms. Whether it's "man-caused disasters" or "workplace violence," our leaders can't stop creating new lies out of old words. Taxing the rich is now "paying our fair share." Class warfare is now called "a war on inequity." As I've said before, calling the Fort Hood massacre workplace violence is like calling Pearl Harbor an air show.

I keep waiting for the day they start calling rain "solar moisture," as a way to somehow link it to global warming. And will it be too long before child molestation is called "impatient courtship"? After all, wasn't their only crime that they just couldn't wait?

Where does this all come from? Hurt feelings. We have an administration fearful of making people feel bad.

Consider the space program (or what's left of it). President Obama sees NASA not as just a place for technological innovation and achievement but also a great place to help Muslims feel good about being Muslim. At one point his administration suggested that the space program was one way to raise self-esteem among followers of the Koran. Called "outreach," it's something you normally see in youth soccer games, where the weaker players are forced to play a half a game even if it means your team loses (worse, they still get their fair share of orange slices). Can you imagine if this mentality infected the medical sciences? Instead of finding cures for disease, we'd be focused on how the doctors felt about medical school, and all those intense pressures to, you know, study and achieve. Better let the very worst doctors operate on you. Who cares if you die from a simple appendectomy? At least the doctor felt included!

Intolerance for achievement is masked as tolerance for difference. It's more important that the astronauts or the hospital staff look diverse than that they actually be any good. I know it's entirely possible for both aims to be accomplished, but trying to aim for diversity over excellence is a recipe for failure—and in some areas of work, death. Want proof it's pure hypocrisy? Let me ask you this: Would Obama get in a space shuttle piloted by someone whose science and math teachers were termed "scholastically challenged"?

We overlook the fact that pushing an inept person in a realm where they can be more inept only makes their lives worse. Better to put them in a place where they do the least amount of damage (like hosting a show on Current TV).

At the heart of all of this is a deliberate dismissal of exceptionalism, in favor of tolerance. Remember when President Obama was asked if he believed in American exceptionalism, he said, sure—just as Greeks would believe in Greek exceptionalism and so on. So really what he said was: Everyone believes in exceptionalism, which means there *is no such thing as exceptionalism*. What has replaced the belief that America is the greatest country in the world? Well, that America is the most "tolerant" country in the world. After Bush, being liked meant so much more than being feared. Hence the push for Muslims in space. Hey, maybe a functioning Islamic Earth program would be a good idea first.

In Obama's mind, tolerance is far more valuable and wonderful than superiority. It's better to be liked, and to like everyone, than to be number one. In the end, that's the real crime of tolerance: it's used as a ceiling on achievement relegating the U.S. to being just another country. And you see the aftereffects of that in the Middle East revolutions of early 2011. What most Americans might expect from their leader is more than a mildly worded statement condemning certain behaviors. But we barely got that. Instead of leading the world, we gawked. We are now exactly what Obama envisioned: not a leader of the free world but just another inhabitant on a planet—observing the wrath of assholes in Syria with a dispassionate distaste one might have for a loud party happening across the street. The fact is, Obama got more upset about the cop who arrested Henry Louis Gates than he did about the shit going down in Iran. Maybe he should have asked Ahmadinejad to a beer summit. I bet the little ingrate wouldn't even bring a bag of pretzels.

TO OBAMA, BORDERS WAS NOTHING BUT A BOOKSTORE

THE FIRST THING THEY DO WHEN anyone starts a country is draw lines on a map. Guess what? We did it, too. But thanks to tolerance, America is the only nation in human history not allowed to have one of those border thingies. Mexico gets one. Several, in fact. Can we have just one? When do we get to call bullshit on the rest of the world and get to have a border? But that would place citizens over noncitizens in the American pecking order—which is utterly intolerant.

And so you have an exercise in revulsion, directed at the state of Arizona, which was only trying to figure out this crap for itself. By simply trying to enforce the laws that the feds are too scared to enforce (God forbid they appear racist or even judgmental), they've become painted as intolerant bigots. And this is fueled by our own government, waving their spindly, cowardly finger at the governor and her fed-up constituents. It gets so bad that even when tragedy strikes (the Tucson shooting), the media sees fit to blame Arizona for it, not a crazed maniac. That's because if you actually believe in something as simple as borders, you must be intolerant—and in the eyes of opportunistic leftists, it was that climate of hate over immigration that made the shooting possible.

This logic extends to the most ridiculous of places, and I say that as I pop an extra-strength Mucinex, which requires a form of ID to purchase. It's true. When I go and buy cough or cold medicine, I have to do what everyone else does: present some sort of picture ID so everyone can make sure I'm actually me. Thankfully, I still have my club card from Teddy Bear Village ("the best place for hugs"), and it still gets me into various places with minimal effort. But I don't make a fuss about rummaging for the card, even though I know the process is, on the whole, pointless when it's directed at me. Presenting ID for Mucinex or Sudafed or whatever is based on the fact that a lot of people buy the stuff to make crystal meth—a drug I've never tried, but I've heard it does wonders for your teeth. Frankly, having to buy tons of over-the-counter remedies to make one under-the-counter drug seems like a lot of work. I stick to simple processes, like lying to my doctor about my unbearable back pain.

But among the many other mundane things in life I've learned to do without thinking too much is to always have my ID. To me, it's like changing my sheets—something I do at least every two weeks. At forty-seven, I still get carded once in a while in bars, mainly because it's customary for a bouncer to card everyone in order to keep his job, and that includes a middle-aged man in leather cutoffs.

So we live in a world where it's completely tolerated, and acceptable, that you have photo identification for some Kabuki-style "everyone is the same" crowd control. It's the post-9/11 world—and it's the least you can do to offer some peace of mind to everyone else who has to put up with your shifty demeanor and furtive manner in public.

Well, what if you want to do something that's pretty important, like vote? Shouldn't you have an ID? Isn't that what one would call a reasonable request? You need an ID to buy cigarettes, why not to cast a ballot—which is every bit as important as inhaling a Salem while riding on the back of a lawnmower you've nicknamed Squatdevil.

Not if you're Eric Holder, or the administration he works for. In 2011, the Justice Department determined that the provisions of South Carolina's Act R54, which would require voters to show photo identification to vote, is unconstitutional—for the state. In Holder's angry muddled mind, South Carolina has not proven the law will not have "a discriminatory effect on minority voters." Never mind that in a few other states where IDs are required, voting participation *went up.* That's not the issue, of course. You are a racist—case closed. Holder has also done the same thing with Texas, again ignoring the fact that voting participation skyrocketed among blacks and Hispanics in Georgia once IDs were made available.

Talk about the soft bigotry of low expectations. Does Holder really believe minorities are incapable of getting a voter ID? The underlying notion is insidious, for it says you can't depend on minorities to get photo identification. You're just asking too much of them. You get a photo ID from Costco, for chrissake. Not that I really noticed, but thinking about it now, I'm pretty sure I see plenty of minorities in plenty of places where you need an ID.

And while Holder finds the idea of presenting IDs to vote a violation of your rights, he seems okay with the idea when you want to pay him a visit. As Robert Bluey pointed out in a harmless, modest stunt, you need a photo ID to visit the Department of Justice (which he did, without an appointment). He also pointed out, during this mini-exposé, that the groups supporting the crusade against voter ID laws (Center for American Progress and the Lawyers' Committee for Civil Rights Under Law) require IDs to enter the building. At the LCCRUL (great acronym, guys), there's even a sign, Bluey notes, that reads ALL VISITORS MUST SHOW ID.

As always, if the tolerati doesn't like what you're doing—even if they're not sure why—they are convinced it's got to be racist. And yep, simply by requiring a photo identification so someone might vote means you are prejudiced against nonwhite people. Or even dead people, for that matter, who seem to be emerging as a valuable constituency for the Democratic Party. In fact, it's gotten nauseating how the left panders to the dead. This special interest stuff has got to stop.

So why does this reasoning only apply to voting and not to any other kind of process that requires flashing an ID? If a liquor store owner asks a Mexican for his ID when he's buying a beer, is that racist, too? If a Mexican family is going to see a PG-17 film, would requiring the kids to show ID cross the line? What if I just went on Mexican TV and cooked myself naked into a burrito? That makes about the same sense.

One of the primary arguments against IDs is that they cost money, and that's, in effect, a poll tax. I'm no expert, but I've read up on this stuff, and I've found that IDs are becoming free, if they're not free already. What costs money is the stuff you need to do to get the ID—like a copy of a birth certificate, which may set you back 25 bucks (less than half of a monthly cell phone bill, I reckon). The other stuff—your Social Security card and proof of residence—is free. But these are just "untenable burdens" in the long line of "untenable burdens" that the tolerati find unacceptable. ID cards are just like birth control: liberals have no sense of modulation, so everything is grossly unfair or a hardship. But something tells me if you can't scrounge up 25 bucks for a copy of your birth certificate, you're probably two years old and ineligible to vote—or you're dead. And if you're dead, again, you can't vote, unless you're a Democrat and "live" in a swing state.

This kerfuffle (which sounds like an adorable marsupial baked into a flaky turnover) is actually emblematic of a bigger idea—an idea that says a commonsense concern over strong borders and legal immigration is emblematic of a sinister form of racism. That if you believe everyone should follow the same laws, you are actually singling out a group perceived to be incapable of following those rules. Like illegal immigrants—who, by virtue of being illegal (and to some it is a virtue), do not have an authentic ID. So asking them for an ID is evil, mean-spirited, and intolerant. And it's a sort of behavior that shall not be tolerated by the tolerant Democrats. Imagine if a flight attendant had to ask you if you were capable of handling the responsibilities that accompany sitting in the emergency exit row, and you couldn't. Is that the flight attendant's fault? According to Holder, it would be. And how weird is it that leftists call a law requiring IDs for voting illegal, but then claim you can't call illegals illegal?

Here's one irony I enjoy breaking to liberals: Your favorite country, France, enforces its borders like you wouldn't believe. Ever go through a French border crossing? Dressed as a woman, and you're late for dinner? It makes the TSA look like the welcome wagon. (Note: What the hell is a welcome wagon, anyway? Has anyone ever actually seen one? Should that be the new name for our immigration policy?) The Gallic socialist paradise is about as interested in taking in undocumented people as it is in scarfing down hot dogs or creating tolerable pop music. But because they "support their artists" through a rapacious tax rate, the French get a pass and are allowed to have a border. (Strangely, it's a right they waive as soon as someone shows up with a couple of tanks. I kid the French.) Why is America then the Great Satan? Because we try to make the place just slightly harder to get into than your average Mets–Astros game?

Tolerance is an amazing thing, for it allows all sorts of behavior, except those that seem innocuous. How is presenting a photo ID so evil? No one can actually explain it, which is why they prefer the race card over your basic library card. If someone has an ID, then that means they're a citizen, and can vote. If you don't have an ID, you should probably get one. If you don't want to get one—because you're a criminal or here illegally—that's not our problem, that's yours. You can still rip us off left and right, and we know you probably will. Or you may work your ass off for wages that should be significantly higher. Those are other issues. But either way, tough noogies. You can't vote. And if you're scared of getting an ID, then that says something about your motives, and not mine. Although, on the whole, I wish I never had to use an ID. It's from six years ago, and, in retrospect, the braids I got at Club Med seem like a bad idea.

WORKING AT THE DEATH STAR

"YOU SHOULD PROBABLY TAKE THAT DOWN."

Those were the words of my adorable Realtor, in my bedroom, after I gestured toward a framed newspaper featuring yours truly on the cover. The article inside *The Observer* covered my new, highly improbable career as a talk show host on a network reviled by the basic lefty Manhattanite. The headline was something like "Watch Out, Jon Stewart," and it featured a delightful drawing of my sweaty face.

It had to go. Quickly.

It was like a swastika, a Confederate flag, or a corpse nailed to the wall—offensive, smelly, and a threat to property values.

See, the Mrs. and I were selling our apartment, in New York, and it had occurred to all of us that there were more than a few things on the walls, coffee tables, and bookshelves that might upset a potential buyer. That newspaper was one, but there were other things, too.

Books, mainly. Books by Ann Coulter. Books by Mark Steyn. Books on unicorn dressage. A few books by me. (I keep them around as gifts, because I'm cheap.) Essentially, all of these things had to go, because they expressed one scary idea: a right-winger lives here. He sleeps on that bed, where he probably does horrible things. To kids, to puppies, to kids with puppies.

Yep. A conservative. Not a liberal. An evil, baby-eating fascist Bu$$$Hitler fanatic who probably is secretly gay while bullying gay teens on the way to school. Better fumigate this place before we sell it. It's got KKKooties.

Although it's an almost accurate description of me (minus the secretly-gay-bullying-gay-teen thing), this fact might hinder our goal of selling our Hell's Kitchen pad and moving to some place quieter—a neighborhood not littered with people I propositioned at four a.m.

Normally, I don't care if anyone sees what I read, or what I've written (which is a great benefit to me when I receive my royalty check). Over time, as I worked among libs for most of my life, my skin has become thicker than a high school yearbook.

But when you parade New Yorkers into your house, and you want them to shell out a pile of dough on a tiny plot of land in a grimy block surrounded by methadone-heads, you will do what-ever it takes to close the deal. Even if that means removing every offending book, magazine, or three-headed vibrator with my name on it. God forbid one of these potential buyers, in their $800 Oliver Peoples glasses, should spy something that isn't in lockstep with their worldview (which is why the vibrators stayed).

The hallucinating "street poet" on our corner who feels his nuclear spittle is universally accepted currency? No effect on property values. One issue of *Reason* on an end table? Could be a problem!

Now, since it is New York, it's not that I expect people to know who I am. It's not like I'm Rachel Maddow, the patron saint of the smirking left. But we couldn't take that chance. Because it really isn't "me" anyway that upsets people. It's who I work for. Yep, I work at the Death Star, the fair and balanced joint that's beating the crap out of its competitors. For a liberal, my network symbolizes everything they hate, even if they couldn't find it on their channel guide to save their life. It's a handy reference point whenever they get angry but can't think of anything to say. When flummoxed at a protest, they realize condemning the network will get them out of any jam, without ever having to say anything that might require actual intelligence.

My theory on why my employer has become the go-to device when griping about the right: it's better than saying "my parents." Because the network is wildly popular among their parents—your parents too—and even their parents (otherwise known as grandparents). I've noticed when someone rails on the network to me it takes about ten minutes before they confess, "It's on all the time at my mom's place." One time I had asked a young dude to do my show, and he informed me, instantly, that he "fucking hates it." A week later, a friendlier response dropped into my e-mail inbox. Turns out his "teabagging mom" loves what I do. And now he wanted in, because it made her so damn happy. But time had passed, and I was now trying to book a man who could juggle cats. Cats who play the piano. You ever see one of those videos? You think they're real? That's a really talented family!

So when you see someone who hates my place of work, bear in mind not to condemn his or her family. Chances are he really means he hates his mom and dad for something (they never let him win at KerPlunk), and that same mom and dad dig the "fair and balanced" way of things.

It's really no wonder they hate the network. So much so, some want to shut the place down. Which is the beauty of modern tolerance. Freedom of expression and tolerating points of view are their expressed desires . . . unless you, um, disagree with them on something. Then it's sooo over, you Nazi!

You remember the Fairness Doctrine? This harebrained notion

percolates up every now and then from the deeper reaches of the left's fever swamps. The idea is to "balance" the right's presence on talk radio with more radio networks from the left. Or something like that. Never mind that every liberal radio network that's tried to compete in the open market has gone over like a Manson family reunion. So what does the tolerant left propose? What they always propose: legislation. Let's force the country to listen to cloying liberal chat hosts in the name of "equal" time.

I practically say it in my sleep these days: For decades the left owned the playing field, the ball, the audience, and the refs. They owned the game we call media. All major networks. All entertainment options came saddled with their approved assumptions: Movies, theater, the art world, magazine publishing, newspapers, comedians, poetry readings in coffeehouses, hopscotch tournaments, the world knitting conference, the Pencak Silat World Invitational (which I won last year)—you name it—they all uniformly turn left as if they're participating in an ideological NASCAR event. The media was the big boys; we were just incidental characters, satiated by cheese puffs and fluffernutters. Until one monster entered the picture, like the Creature emerging from the Black Lagoon. Yep, just one single company refused to go lockstep with them—an unafraid horde with its chin out and every bit as much intellectual heft as its adversaries, and they couldn't take it. Even the president can't resist griping about it. It's just not as "real" as those *Entourage* reruns he loves to DVR.

Back to my inane sports metaphor: When this new media entity showed up, the left wanted to take their ball and go home. Tolerance for others stopped at 1211 Avenue of the Americas, where this weirdo whose book you're currently reading abides and steals its toilet paper.

So what is the argument for not tolerating another voice? Well, it's all in the spirit of tolerance. See, because the left identifies me as evil (or rather, different), it's okay not to tolerate me. Tolerating me would be like tolerating murder, bestiality, or soft jazz— but worse, because, you know, I'm a right-winger. Which again is really shorthand for "Daddy, who never gave me the hug or an adult allowance."

But if you watch any one of my shows for even ten minutes, you realize they have loads of lefties on. We tolerate the left because it's part of our mission—to be fair and balanced. I know the left snickers at that, but realize that it would be idiotic not to present both left and right opinions. Fact is, because I don't reflexively reflect the shared opinions of contemporary progressive thought, I have a target on my back. Which means I have to be that much more charitable. Because I am confident in my mission, presenting liberal perspectives should only make whatever else that much stronger. Seriously, put a leftist on any show and you see how much more sensible the right is. You have me sitting there sounding reasonable and anyone to my left morphs into one of those LSD experiments from the fifties, even if I'm not wearing pants.

In the kiddie pool that is tolerance, my side wins hands down over MSNBC, CNN, and every other media entity you can mention. But it doesn't matter—the left will only deny it, justifying their own bitter attacks against this big fat meanie. And boy do they hate that meanie, so much so that they cannot watch it (which is another point: ask a critic what show they can't stand and why, and you realize they never watch it—they just assume it's evil). They assume the whole channel is evil. It's like the world's biggest factory for child slavery.

Which leads me to this morning (it's October 30, 2011, for you people totally into dates and numbers). It's an odd Sunday morning. I'm going to lay it out for you from the beginning, so you can see why it's important. And because this is a story about Twitter, it will involve tweets. But I hate reading stories where the tweets interrupt the flow, so I will be paraphrasing a lot of this to save time and keep your attention from straying to other things (like my nude Pilates videos).

I currently wrote about this on my website, the Daily Gut, but in case you missed it: Last night (a wintry Saturday), some weird dude tweets me—in CAPS. I don't know why crazy people don't see that typing in CAPS reveals their seething instability, but I guess that's a circular argument one can never escape from. If you ask them if they're crazy, they respond, I'M NOT CRAZY!!! I'M NOT CRAZY!!! Anyhoo, he calls me a wannabe "f*ckface." No big deal. I retweet it with a comment, "Mom, we've had this discussion."

I continue drinking into the stormy night at a local steakhouse. I go to bed. While I'm asleep, some dude (dudette?) on Twitter, pretending to be me, with a fake account, tweets to the creepy all-CAPS dude—calling him a "faggot."

The Twitter account is obviously fake, but sensing a glorious opportunity to destroy me, the all-CAPS dude vows he's going to ruin my life by spreading that tweet everywhere.

And he sets out to do so, with great zest. Sunday morning, I wake up and look at my laptop. There are three "Google alerts," telling me something. I hate Google alerts, but I also love them. In a way, they're like children who jump on your bed demanding to go to the zoo. Except this zoo is filled with bad news instead of bad gnus. (Note to reader: I should turn off my laptop and simply retire. I will never write a line greater than that.)

The first one is from a website, Back2Stonewall, claiming I

tweeted something homophobic. I click to the next alert, and this one scares me. It's The Raw Story, a major left-wing site, also reporting that I tweeted something homophobic. They were more charitable, though, unlike the Stonewall folks, who referred to me as a homophobic shit-weasel. I am not sure what a shit-weasel is, but I'm thinking it's not a compliment.

I head over to Twitter. There, Back2Stonewall has tweeted this slur not once, but four times. Apparently lost in the glee of capturing a conservative in full homophobic glory, he neglects to e-mail or call anyone for verification (which is the first thing you learn in any journo course), or click over to the fraudulent Twitter account, to see that it's false.

And believe me, even my mom could see it was fake. The guy took advantage of a typography flaw in Twitter, where an upper-case *I* looks like a lower-case *L*. So he spelled "gutfeld," as "gutfeId." And if you look to the right, you'll see he isn't verified and doesn't have a long history of tweeting. Or followers. He has a handful of followers and a handful of tweets—all of them nonsense (or more nonsensical than mine). It was obviously a dummy account.

Anyway, that didn't concern Back2Stonewall. He boasted that he had screen grabs of my offensive tweet, which he claims had been taken down by me; but oddly he left out the entire screen grab, which would have shown the very low tweet/follower numbers.

Why did he do that? I don't know. Maybe, in haste, he didn't see the whole screen. Or maybe, because the story was just too good to be true, it didn't matter if it wasn't.

I contacted a lawyer, a high-powered gentleman with an office near the perfume counter at Macy's. Then I contacted the Back2Stonewall guy and the dude at Raw Story. The blogger at Raw

Story acted fast, and fixed it, and thanked me. The Back2Stonewall website never responded to me. So I hit him up on Twitter.

He reacted differently from the Raw Story guy—saying he wasn't sure if my story was true, and besides, evil right-wingers don't verify stuff either (if only that were true, my life would be a lot simpler). It infuriated me. Instead of looking at the facts, he adopted a stereotypical, ideological stance, basically saying, "Yeah, it's not true, but since I don't like you, I don't care."

I tweeted to everyone that this was a hoax, and also engaged the Stonewall fellow, asking him to put aside ideology and do the right thing. I sent him the facts. I posted the screen grabs of the fake account. But I could tell it was hard for him—he wanted so badly for me to be a right-wing homophobe, so much so that he couldn't let go of the lie. It was like trying to deprogram a Raëlian who tweets.

His jab at my network revealed something else: That a lie is permissible if it serves a greater good. Because I work for "the enemy," it doesn't matter if I really didn't post that offensive tweet, because I'm evil anyway. I'm sure lefties think that I probably agree with the sentiment of that tweet, even if I didn't write it. Despite the fact that I've been called that very epithet. By the left, on Twitter.

I filed a complaint with Twitter, and monitored Twitter and Google to see where the story was going. After some time, Back2Stonewall retracted the story, saying also that they sincerely regretted publishing it. But embroidered in the apology was a nonapology—that while B2S was embarrassed by being fooled, I should be embarrassed by my followers. B2S also tweeted, sarcastically, what a "great f*cking day" it had been—as if he were the victim in all this.

Fact is, it is sad that I have to feel grateful Raw Story and Stone-wall retracted the phony story. I should feel outrage that they ran with it to begin with. I mean, how hard is it to contact me? Google my name, and you end up at my website, the Daily Gut. I'm on Twitter! I respond. I am that lonely.

Perhaps they chose not to contact me because they didn't think they needed to—clearly, someone like me would say something that bigoted on Twitter, so why bother verifying? Also, if I denied it, there goes the story. And besides, if I wasn't guilty of this, so what? I'm guilty of so much else. I've got it coming, you know (which I do, but for reasons more related to a spring break in the 1990s than for what these knuckleheads contend).

Like I said, the blind acceptance of the story is worse than the fraudulent tweet. And, really, that's why I'm writing this now—to explain to a few of you why this is a big deal. If I hadn't jumped on this accusation first thing, I would have been destroyed, outnum-bered by every left-wing website feeding off a prior link to that original website, building a tower of proof that I am a homophobe who should be fired. I feared that the fake account would disap-pear and then I would really be screwed.

Some people might say, "Dude, it's Twitter. Lighten up." But those people are fools. Once it got on Raw Story, it would be on the HuffPo, then the New York media sites, then MSNBC, etc. I had to kill it before the caterpillar became a butterfly (which is generally my approach to caterpillars and butterflies).

So, back to the apartment. Yeah, the East Coast liberals looking at real estate must really hate people like me. And I have to sell my apartment, so I have to get myself out of the "I hate conservatives" equation. I have to erase my existence in my 900-square-foot apartment. Because I don't really believe a lefty—no matter how much they love the apartment, in a New York real estate market that remains highly competitive—would buy a place inhabited by someone who, in their mind, probably eats the homeless (I do).

In real estate sections of city magazines, you'll occasionally come across a feature on an agent whose job it is to sell houses where grisly crimes took place. Suicide, drug overdoses, mass murder, dance parties hosted by Bob Schieffer—all of these lower the price of property, not just for that residence but for the places surrounding it. Debates occur as to whether that information should be disclosed during the selling, or somehow interested buyers should be allowed find out by themselves. Maybe they'll just assume it's a wine stain.

Sadly, I've never seen an article on how to sell your place if you are a well-known righty. Maybe it isn't as big a deal as I think, but I don't know anyone else who has to hide the things they read or write before an open house. Not that I was forced to do it, but it made sense to do it anyway. It's like if I had a bondage fetish, and I had to hide the equipment. It's why I have a false floor under the bed for the fetish clothing and restraints. (I told the contractor it was for Christmas decorations.) I wonder if there is a "conservative lived here" exorcist service? Maybe they can import the Reverend Wright to wave around a copy of *The Nation* and dispel all the evil, righty demons.

I don't think this is an issue for someone working at MSNBC, because, of course, liberal perspectives are embraced by New Yorkers. If you were to take in an open house, and spy a book on a coffee table by Bill Maher, you might throw up, but most Manhattanites would ponder pleasantly how they share the same assumptions as the homeowner. It might even make them more likely to buy—even if they can't afford the place (something that doesn't bother most New Yorkers). *We just deserve to live there! These are my people!*

While we were selling the apartment, we were also looking. And in nearly every place we hit we found the same old crap on coffee tables. Books by Bill Moyers and Al Gore seemed common. I didn't see any copies of *Decision Points* lying around. But it didn't bother me. It's part of the wallpaper. If I buy the place, I ain't buying the stuff that goes with it. One pretty cool apartment I saw had the owner's stuff everywhere. Apparently he created soundtracks to movies, and he had his many awards all over the place. It didn't make me want to buy the place—it just made me feel like the guy who lived there was a show-off. And he could've at least closed his robe during the open house.

And it wasn't like I tried to get a job as a talking head whose role is to challenge the left. Remember, I was a fitness editor—for *Prevention* magazine! The magazine that made *Reader's Digest* look hip. I taught old people how to do sit-ups on cruise ships. I was also editor of *Men's Health.* Then *Stuff,* and finally *Maxim.* These are not stepping stones to conservative punditry. Nope. I was sequestered in magazine publishing, a bastion of stifling liberalism so mundane in belief that for everyone in the profession, politics doesn't even come up. The assumptions are such a given, it's almost impossible for them to see the point of debate.

Being an open conservative in publishing is akin to being a gay communist in 1950s Nebraska.

They would find out my dirty secret by accident. Sitting in the cafeteria, everyone laughing about another stupid Republican, they'd see I wasn't joining in. Instead I'd be lost in thought, stabbing an overcooked baked potato. And they'd ask why I didn't find Newt's latest gaffe hilarious. And then it would unfold: First, they would assume I was joking when I disagreed with them. Then, when they realized I was serious, they were confused. The kind of confusion you see on the face of a puppy watching a clothes dryer. The stages were as predictable as the ones for grief. Then, for the rest of my career there, I became "that guy." The coldhearted right-winger with a dungeon full of delicious orphans.

The good news is that when my political views spread around that company, like-minded strangers would pop out of the woodwork. They would stop by my office to chat. The president of Rodale Press suddenly became a close friend—a telling fact that the most powerful person in the building was a righty. In that company, possessing over a thousand employees, there were maybe ten of us. Which is nine more than I expected. We would meet in the basement, at night. Using a secret password: "Morey Amsterdam." (Don't ask me why—and if you ask anyone else about this they'll just deny everything. That was part of our pact.)

Where I work now, there are plenty of outspoken righties. But there are also tons of lefties. There are also lots of gays and greenies. There, everything is tolerated, so much more than at all the other "open-minded" places I toiled in.

My employer is so tolerant, in fact, that it saves lives. I end this chapter on a surreal note: Sitting at lunch with the staff of one of my shows in a tony Midtown steakhouse. At the table sat an immensely lovable, colorful, hard-charging, cantankerous lefty known for running the Dukakis campaign and working in the Carter administration, among other things. He's a bright man, whose views can veer from sharp to delightfully incoherent within the same sentence. During the appetizers, he went blue. Then purple. He was choking to death on an oversized shrimp (not me). The first one up at the table? The boss. This most evil of evil right-wingers pulled the lefty out of his chair and administered the Heimlich like a seasoned paramedic. Progress was made, but something was still stuck in the poor guy's throat, and a fellow cohost—bigger and with longer arms—jumped over the table and finished the Heimlich successfully, and the lefty was saved by a righty.

Yep, a righty saved a lefty. But don't read too much into it, or you might think conservatives aren't so bad after all. It's like finding out Darth Vader was your father.

A PACK OF LIES

SO I'M SMOKING A CIGARETTE on the corner near my apartment when I hear two girls behind me, heckling me. Like I'm playing third base for the Phillies, which I imagine is a sports team made of adorable horses. At any rate, they're loud. The girls, that is.

"Get lung cancer, man."

"Secondhand smoke, asshole."

"Hope you get cancer."

I did my best to ignore it. But they kept going, getting louder and louder and saying all sorts of crap. (I think they might have had Tourette's.) Finally, in a monumental moment of stupidity, I turned around and asked them, logically, "Why are you doing this?"

They said, "Cuz it's secondhand smoke. You're going to die." I stupidly tried to explain how that really doesn't work outside.

Secondhand smoke may be the most exaggerated panic since global warming, attention deficit disorder, bird flu, and Yahtzee combined. But because smokers are the easiest target to project your instant outrage onto, no one really questions it anymore.

I joked to the girls that they were getting more toxic stuff from the bus billowing exhaust nearby. But sensing they had a hapless participant in their afternoon volley of acceptable bullying, they started once again, saying they wanted me to die.

Now, I left out the part that these girls were black. By the way, there were plenty of black people on Ninth Avenue also smoking. That's the thing about smoking—everyone does it. It's a unifier. The great equalizer. A good lung dart has brought more people together than Kofi Annan singing Kumbaya. Addiction is color blind. It's like stupidity. The reason this is important is that as a middle-aged white-guy smoker, I will lose, on paper, and elsewhere, when engaging in a debate with two young black women. In the name of modern political correctness, I must tolerate the abuse of strangers, even if I'm innocent. These delightful young lasses, however, could come after me with a vengeance. And, again, I didn't want to end up on NY1 News (I was in pajamas under my coat) because my appropriate response would be construed as a racial attack.

I kept walking and they followed me, harassing me even more, even louder. Finally, I snapped, turned around, told them to fuck themselves, and tossed my cig.

The damn thing bounced. And nearly landed on their feet.

They came for me. For a brief, ugly moment, I thought my life was heading for total and complete ruin. Surely, I would be attacked, a crowd would form around me, chanting "Racist, racist, pajama-wearing racist," and ultimately I would be arrested. My face would be all over the news, with clever headlines like "Butt-Loving Bigot." I'd have to publicly apologize, shed tears in a press conference, and enter private one-on-one counseling with a man named after an herb. I'd get an earring and make PSAs against bullying. I'd denounce patriarchy and gender oppression, then call for reparations and a new currency based on the likenesses of dead hip-hop artists. I would confess I was a victim of adolescent beatings, and also a bisexual hustler during college. I would claim I was molested by an overfamiliar emu at the zoo as a child (which is b.s.; he was just being polite, although he still sends me flowers on my birthday). I would reveal my addiction to snorting pixie sticks in public toilets with Pauly Shore. In prime time, Dr. Drew would hold me while I shook with tears.

This horror fantasy was way too much to bear. I scurried off into a drugstore and hid behind an *Us Weekly* (where I was gratified to learn that Elton John and his husband, David Furnish, had adopted either a child or a member of the Kardashian family—I was understandably distracted at the time, and possibly drunk).

My point is, I had three strikes against me: I am white, I am male, and I was smoking. The girls had three strikes for them: they were young, female, and black. I realized that no matter how this "debate" would unfold, I would probably be the bad guy. I was already deemed bad. In the world of tolerance, I had no protective force field against ready-made rage—but they did. It's an uncomfortable truth, but so be it. I guess this was payback for four hundred years of oppression that I keep hearing about but had nothing to do with it.

If only this were an isolated incident, regarding my smoking habit.

I smoke—not a lot, but I smoke. And I smoke outside, which puts me in the vicinity of other people—primarily nonsmokers, who are usually pleasant people as long as they don't talk to me. Sometimes, when they get drunk, they start hitting me up for cigarettes, looking at me as if I am some weird cigarette tree, which they can freely grab a smoke from whenever they're tipsy. (As a rule, I never give out cigs to strangers—especially in New York, where it's fast approaching a buck a cigarette. I look at cigs like I look at birth control—you can buy your own—unless you're Sandra Fluke.)

But here's an experiment I undertook to illustrate how some behaviors are tolerated over others. I'm sitting outside at the hotel bar of this new joint in Hell's Kitchen. It's got a beautiful wraparound terrace, and I'm lounging at a table, with no intention of smoking. The signs plainly say "no smoking," and I'm anything but a lawbreaker. I'll happily go downstairs to the street to puff. The exercise is fantastic for sculpting quads.

The bar is sparsely attended. In fact, it's pretty much empty, but clean and laid-back, the sun creeping down as night approaches. I sit for twenty minutes waiting for a server to get my first drink. Then thirty minutes. It's now forty-five minutes and no one is waiting on me. Perhaps they're too busy handicapping the Tonys. So I look to my friend and say, "Watch this." I light up a cig. I take a drag, and instantaneously, I have a bartender, a waitress, a manager, and a bouncer at my left side. In unison, they tell me, "There is no smoking here." It was then I said, "I know. I just wanted service, and smoking was the only way to get your attention." They seemed peeved at my cleverness—and took my drink order. I'm sure they wrote, "Asshole at table 7" on my check. But after getting my drink, and drinking it, the same thing happened: After an hour, no service in sight. If I had suffered a coronary, I would have died on the spot. What I couldn't understand: Why were we getting no service but there were waiters everywhere? Did I forget to change my underwear? The answer is yes, but that wasn't the issue. They seemed to be in some sort of complex dance, a floating ritual of purposeless behavior involving serving trays, gossip, and ice. Otherwise known as "New York service industry hipsters and the ennui they've embraced." Also known as: lazy.

So I looked to my friend and said, "One more time." And sure enough, holding the cigarette was enough. It wasn't even lit, and I had the cavalry of angry servers. This time they weren't polite, and the manager scolded me. I replied, "If you were a decent manager, this wouldn't happen. You care more about smokers than service, you bozo." Because the manager was not from New York—or the country, for that matter—he took *bozo* to mean something pejorative, far worse than it was, and I was escorted out by some beefy men. My friend stayed back (traitor that he is) and noticed everyone there was shaken by the incident.

All over smoking.

I haven't been back there since, which sucks, because it's a beautiful spot. But there are lots of beautiful spots, and some of them "tolerate" smoking, even if the city doesn't. The one bright spot about the shitty economy: the city has given up being a nuisance, and looks the other way if someone is smoking at a café table if it helps business. We just don't have the luxury of fining people over a behavior whose illegality is based on faulty science and people's phony outrage over something they don't do.

That's the crux of antismoking intolerance. People can rag on smokers because smoking is not in their life. Even if they know my smoking has no effect on them (and it doesn't—anyone who spends an hour researching secondhand smoke or, now, "thirdhand" smoke will find more holes in the data than in my mesh workout shorts), they still love getting their back up to express concern for families in the vicinity of my evil, evil smoke. It's easy, fun outrage. Fact is, we have so few times in our lives to be justifiably outraged—to flex our "angry" muscles—that many leap at the opportunity to nail an easy target like some dude smoking Parliaments. It's either that or join an "angry" gym to keep the anger muscles in shape. If they don't exist, perhaps someone should invent them.

And this stupid, phony outrage is even infecting campuses. As reported by CNN in the summer of 2011, a group of University of Kentucky students and faculty began going around the campus grounds looking for anyone who might be smoking. The Tobacco-free Take Action volunteers police the area, approaching smokers and asking them to stop. I wonder what I would do if an undergrad with purple hair in a PETA shirt told me to put out a cigarette. I'd light up and take a drag off an unfiltered Camel, if I had one. Then put it out on his forehead.

I think about this, now that Mayor Bloomberg has instituted a ban on smoking in Times Square (a few touristy blocks from my equally congested apartment, except Times Square has fewer sex workers). When asked how the ban would be enacted, his minions said it would be enforced by citizens—a recipe for fistfights if you ever saw one. In NYC? I can't imagine some spindly Columbia grad students approaching a Russian tourist to ask him to put out his Sobranie. Their eyeballs would end up in the East River.

But the university hall monitors are far worse, in my opinion, for now we have colleges turning students into snitches—instead of encouraging them to do the things they are supposed to do in college (which are . . . I forget). Apparently, the University of Kentucky is one of more than five hundred campuses that have adopted a 100 percent no-tolerance policy, banning smoking on all grounds, including even campus parking lots. If you smoke, you have to go off campus to do it, which often means heading into areas that aren't exactly safe. True, smoking can kill you, but that's fifty or sixty years away. But you can get run over by a drunk at twenty because some policy forced you to smoke behind

THE JOY OF HATE

the dumpster in an alley behind the tattoo joint. (You do meet interesting people there, however. Who really seem to know a lot about modern jurisprudence!) But were it up to me, I'd adhere wholeheartedly to this policy. The University of Kentucky wants me to smoke off campus? Fine, tell you what, guys: Is Ninth Avenue in NYC far enough away? Or should I move to fucking Portugal? Is the University of Kentucky kidding? Go back to mowing bluegrass and jerking off Secretariat and lay off the oppressive social conscience stuff for a while, will ya?

But it makes me wonder: Would campuses ever encourage this kind of intolerance police in the area of, say, unsafe sex? Yep, they do teach safe sex classes, but it's untethered to the moralism you find attached to smoking. If you did that, imagine the outcry. What if a group was formed to police dorms. There would be protests, and cries for dismissal of all involved, followed by some sort of counseling sessions for the victims (because there are always victims).

Fact is, there are only two behaviors that are considered evil in this world—smoking and voting Republican. Wait—also being racist (which describes anyone who votes Republican). Since identifying racists can be hard (they rarely wear the hoods anymore), and Republicans are hiding in plain sight, it falls on smokers to assume the role of target for self-righteous, manufactured rage. You can't hide that thing dangling from your mouth. It's a smoking scarlet letter. I am Hester Prynne!

One last story: I am outside a bar having a cigarette in Los Angeles, standing by potted ferns away from people (in L.A., the two can be tough to tell apart). Within moments of lighting up, I hear a faint "Sir! sir!" from far away. I think it's not directed at me. Despite my brilliant performances on television, my recognition factor tracks somewhere below the likeable folks in the catheter commercials. But then other people start gesturing at me. I squint and I see an older woman and she says, "Could you put that out, please?" She is about 100 feet away. I yell back, "You can't be serious!" She says it bothers her. I say, "Wait. Does the smoke bother you, or does it bother you that I'm smoking?" She looks really confused.

She should be. After all, she lives in a world where she assumes it's okay to assail a stranger about his habits, even if that habit occurs so far away she'd have to hop a taxi to actually experience it. She needed a telescope to see it. But I don't blame her for her assumptions. The world is changing, and thanks to questionable secondhand smoke research, rules are now being enforced that are entirely based on the pleasure of repressive tolerance. We're generating an American caste system, with smokers at the bottom (just under hitmen and NAMBLA members). It's all directed toward one pale sliver of society—a segment of the population who won't fight back because (a) they know smoking is bad, and (b) they are too busy working at a tough job to protest for smokers' rights. See nurses (I do—in my sleep).

Which reminds me: If you're looking for a job these days, you'd better quit smoking. More and more employers (no surprise—a lot of them are hospitals or government agencies) are imposing bans on puffers. The new clichéd sign in the window is NSNA. But if it were up to me, if anyone deserves to smoke, it's a nurse, who has to deal with our gross bodily functions every day. Frankly, any nurse who treats me deserves to smoke for six lifetimes.

But that's just me—I don't run the hospital (thank God— everyone would die). But now companies like the Hollywood Casino in Toledo, Ohio, won't hire you if your pee tests positive for nicotine use—even if the nic comes from electric cigarettes or from patches, or even chewing tobacco. Which I guess means they won't be hiring anyone from major league baseball. Not for nothing, but: Hollywood Casino in Toledo, Ohio? They should be *handing out* cigarettes. And foot massages.

And according to *USA Today,* Idaho's Central District Health Department also voted, in late 2011, to stop hiring smokers. Their reasoning, of course, is that this will reduce bad health practices, which may reduce insurance premiums. I get it. But why stop there? Why not test for cholesterol, or saturated fat, and stop hiring chubbies, who no doubt have higher blood pressure, diabetes risk, and a coating of Cheetos on their fingertips? Is there a blood test for Ho Hos?

At some point, this will happen, when some smart guy—on a government grant—discovers an insidious problem called "secondhand obesity," which finds if you're around a fat person, you're three times more likely to become fat, too. (This research might already exist, but frankly I'm too lazy to look it up and my ice cream might melt in the process.)

According to the Centers for Disease Control and Prevention, smoking or "exposure to secondhand smoke" causes 443,000 deaths per year. See how they did that? I got that number from a *USA Today* article (January 3, 2012). By grouping smoker deaths and secondhand smoker deaths together, they combine the two into one huge number, to make you think the exhaled crap coming out of my mouth is every bit as deadly to you as it is to me (which it probably is—after a night out, my breath could split a tree). That's not just a lie, it's propaganda.

Look, I know what I'm doing is bad for me, but I also know it's not bad for you. The only part that's bad for you is that it is bad for me—and you'll miss me when I'm gone.

You can pass judgment on what I'm doing to myself, but don't pretend I'm infringing on your boring, nonsmoking lifestyle. The fact is, smokers are necessary in order for a wussy culture to find something—anything—to blame. When you've made any and all behaviors perfectly tolerable, you need a scapegoat to spew all that pent-up venom at. So smokers are there to absorb all this nicotine and intolerance, to make a bunch of moral cowards feel good about themselves. We're the tar and disapprobation receptacle. I swear, this secondhand venom has to be dangerous—I can smell it in my clothes. When I publish my study on this ("The Effects of Secondhand Intolerance on the Mental State of the Smoker"), you'll see who has the last laugh. And it will be me. Although I may be coughing instead of laughing.

WINNERS AND LOOTERS

IT WAS LIKE THE OLYMPICS FOR DIRTBAGS. I speak of that chaotic summer of 2011, as rioting in London spread like plaque on rotted teeth. I realized, however, that there was something more toxic than the crazy violence going on. It was the reaction to it, which stank of justification. Says one anarchist, while punks steal chocolate, "This is the uprising of the working class. We're redistributing the wealth" (Fox Nation, August 9, 2011).

Yep, free Mars Bars—that's a revolution.

I'm sure those folks fighting for their lives in Syria and Libya were inspired by your brave fight for a Toblerone.

I'd hate to be a British shopkeeper knowing that the man looting the store is viewed more romantically than the man stocking the shelves.

But you can find this idiocy anywhere: academia, TV, movies, music . . . the belief that despicable behavior is okay if you dress it up as a response to "the man."

But what's worse is the way the media now responds to this crap. It is the curse of political correctness: Our fear of demanding good behavior now allows for bad. And the media is too timid to call it what it is. Repressive tolerance means you can get your head kicked in and you probably had it coming (which you probably did, and don't say I didn't warn you).

Over the course of 2011, I watched this phenomenon called "flash mobs" erupt in various cities—in Philly, especially, but in other places, too, like Milwaukee and Washington, D.C. Every time I pitched the story in our meetings for my show, I knew the segment would always end up in the same place: Why isn't the media covering this stuff?

It could be that maybe this isn't a trend at all. That because of the spread of cell phones with cameras, we happen to catch more bad behavior than before. But it bothered me that I was witnessing something I felt was a direct cause of tolerance—and that somehow it mutated into an accepting mentality that is, at its basic level, inhuman, disgusting. How could we condemn corporate criminals for fleecing investors and not condemn teens doing the same to hardworking people? People who probably came to this country to escape this kind of loathsome behavior?

I realized no one was covering this for the same reason I didn't want to cover it. Fear of being called a bigot.

Could it be that if you expect civilized behavior, you're a racist? Is it better to just look the other way, and lock your doors?

Or move? Some place with a moat?

This was a first step toward something far worse. Letting kids get away with trashing a 7-Eleven and being thankful that they were "orderly" about it makes deviant behavior more acceptable.

Which you saw in the U.K. spread like a virus. A British virus. Like Russell Brand.

And so I must ask, why does looting occur? Well, it happens because you let it. Without fear of punishment, there is no need for the looter to stop, especially when he's got apologists behind him (or her—don't want to offend anyone!).

We know the rioting in England would never happen in Texas.

Personally, I've never met more tolerant people than Texans. They'll let you do just about anything, provided you don't do anything to them. Meaning, "Don't mess with Texas" has an implicit second part to that saying: "and we won't mess with you."

Part of that equation is a threat of harm. You can have all the fun you want, but if you mess with me, I will shoot you in the asshole (that's the Texas "warning shot").

Guns, oddly enough, are the biggest force for real tolerance. If you're a gay cross-dressing cowboy who likes to smoke jazz cigarettes (nothing but the most up-to-date references here, folks) in the privacy of your ranch, a shotgun will protect you from anyone who might find any one of those descriptors objectionable. A gun lets your freak flag fly—provided you don't use that flag to stab someone in the face at a strip mall.

Which is why the U.K. is a mess. Not only are the law-abiding citizens unarmed, but so are the well-meaning cops—who, from my experience living in the place, felt more at home giving directions and taking pictures. Without protections or authority themselves, what's the point of going after the rabble? Let me take a picture of these coeds from Gainesville instead. They have such great teeth (they have teeth).

During the riots, the authors of the smash hit book *Freakonomics* tweeted about a research paper linking recent budget cuts to social unrest in Europe. It claimed, "Once you cut expenditure by more than 2% of GDP, instability increases rapidly . . . especially in terms of riots and demonstrations."

The conclusion: Governments fear austerity programs for this reason. It was, essentially, a threat (or what qualifies as a threat from guys who wear cardigans and tweed jackets).

Meaning riots. Bloodshed. Looting. Kids in ski masks who

aren't skiing at all. And so on. One of the more hilarious out-growths of tolerance: watching politicians debate whether or not they should be able to ask or force these thugs to remove their face masks as they roam the streets looking for flat screens, bags of cat food, and surgical supplies they have no use for. It was an attack on one's freedom, and individuality, to have the audacity to question their garb. You can't find a better consequence of repressive tolerance that endorses the destruction of decency. It's like debating whether a rapist should wear a condom.

So you can't save your city, because the citizens will riot. Which is a sad and scary point: What protects bloated government and entitlement is a visceral fear that if you take candy from the baby, the baby will trash your local supermarket.

Or rather *their* local supermarket. The British looters apparently are so angry, they took it out on the only useful people in their communities, whom they called "rich"—which translates there as "anyone with more than me." Yep, tolerance is a belief that doesn't protect anyone who worked hard for their money. This is why President Obama's "pay your fair share" rhetoric, in the end, was nothing more than stoking the fear of that kind of envy. If you don't agree that the makers should give more to the takers, then the takers might come get you. Commerce is now extortion.

I lived in London (for three years, most of it fat and buzzed), and the cops were great. But without guns, what good are they, besides helping drunks like me back to the tube station before I peed myself? (Which is a vital public service that New York needs to institute.)

But couple that with idiots equating looters to victims and it's no wonder riots continue unabated purely for lurid fun.

Looking at England, we see we've hit the edge of civilization—where, left unprotected, a city will burn, because there is no one impolite enough to prevent it. Letting it happen seems to be all we have left. So we watch it on TV and hope the mob passes us by.

But before I collapse into an existential heap, I want to poop all over this idea that the violence is linked to budget cuts. During the chaos, so many "experts" painted a grim picture of a forgotten generation left without hopes or dreams. Talking heads and scribes mentioned the root causes of the rioters' rage (the killing of a young man by the police), conveniently avoiding the sheer ugliness of these "victims'" behavior.

Yeah. About these victims. It turns out the perps arrested aren't as romantically disenfranchised as the progressive politicians would have wanted. Of course, when the movie is made about all this (and it will be), that won't be the case. The criminals will be gorgeous students with lilting accents, heroic day laborers, poor black DJs—who, fed up with "the man," take the streets back for one glorious week. There will be drugs, sex, and true love occurring among the flames—as two romantic teens unite in sexual congress while the Sony building goes up in smoke. I can't wait to see how Justin Timberlake does with his accent!

In that movie, of course, you won't see the local shopkeepers weeping over the fact that *their neighbors* destroyed their livelihood. You won't see the sheer greed that drove so many to hurt so many others. You also won't see how monumentally stupid and vicious these thugs are. All you will see is Sienna Miller handing out looted Cadbury bars to Welsh coal miners. I only hope that when Oliver Stone directs it, Colin Firth gets run over by a lorry.

That's the movie, but in real life, do you want to know who the "disenfranchised" really were? Here's a short list: a millionaire's daughter, a hairdresser, and a lifeguard.

Yeah, they were all looters, none of whom I'd call a victim of anything other than being an asshole. But my favorite one? An organic chef.

Yep, using pesticides on vegetables is evil, but trashing a restaurant (which is what the chef did) is just "brill" (that's U.K. slang for something).

But who knows, maybe the eatery he targeted used additives in their lamb sausage appetizers! Maybe that breast of chicken didn't once belong to a free-range bird who lived its last moments bathed in music by Enya. For that, they must pay.

My second favorite looter? A female ambassador to the Olympics. At least her mom turned her in (probably to get a reality show). But maybe Mom was wrong and her daughter's looting was for a purpose. Throwing rocks at cops might be great prep for the shot put. Or the next austerity riot.

Remove the false sentimentality and you find no romanticism in the wreckage—only petty selfishness and envy, accelerated by opportunity, greed, and cowardice. And college students who didn't want to take their midterms. It's something you'll see bubbling up again with Occupy Wall Street—justifying riots and assault under the guise of "injustice." What a pathetic world we live in, when even our criminals are a joke. Still, you know England's riots are destined for the Oscars and Danny Boyle's mantelpiece. Which still won't make up for his horrible 2012 Olympic ceremonies. What was that anyway—*Chitty Chitty Bang Bang* for the clinically insane? It must have been, because I loved it.

THE PIRATES OF PENANCE

I HAVE AN IDEA FOR A NEW GAME SHOW called *Ruin Your Life.* In this competition, contestants try to see who can ruin their life the fastest. It's kind of like *Survivor,* but in reverse. The winner is defined by how low their career, personal life, and bank account sink in the shortest amount of time. And more important, none of this can be repaired. Your life is over, even if your heart's still beating.

You'd think right off the bat developing a drug habit would be the way to go. Get addicted to meth, and in a matter of months you look like a living scarecrow, in the back of a car, writing for the Huffington Post.

But there's a much faster way to ruin your life, to lose your job, your friends, your family, your reputation: say something racist, or perceived as racist.

Let's take Michael Richards, a well-known comedic actor who enjoyed a long TV career. I remember him from that *Saturday Night Live* rip-off called *Fridays* back in the 1980s (which, for reasons I could never understand, aired on Fridays). But he made his mark as the daffy Cosmo Kramer on *Seinfeld.* He spent years making an idiot of himself and ultimately a fortune. His success didn't happen overnight, but his downfall did.

All it took was a bizarre outburst on stage, back in November 2006. According to my researcher (his name is Wikipedia), at the Laugh Factory in Hollywood, he dealt with a pair of black hecklers by shouting, "He's a nigger!" to the audience—surely a comedy first. All of this got captured by cell phones.

And that was it. His career vanished like a Rob Schneider film, replaced with a permanent stain. Despite making public apologies by phone to Jerry Seinfeld on the *Late Show with David Letterman,* his goose wasn't just cooked. It was cremated.

So what do you do when you can't dig yourself out of a hole like that? Since one racist incident makes you a racist, surpassing leprosy in achieving total isolation, you've only one recourse: "retire." I.e., scram. Generally to someplace humid and without many televisions. Which is what Richards did, heading off to Cambodia and assorted temples in the search of "spiritual healing" (translation: where Perez Hilton won't find me). I get why he did it: Whenever you screw up, striving for healing, followed by some courses in raising awareness, tends to get you some gentle applause on *The View.* But once you yell the N-word a handful of times, to be seen by everyone, even that bullshit won't fly. Especially with a pissed off Whoopi Goldberg sitting next to you.

Richards isn't the only celebrity to spout racial crap and get nailed for it.

Do you remember Doug "the Greaseman" Tracht? If you never heard of him, it's a good thing. He was once one of the country's most successful, unfunny drive-time shock jocks—until, in 1999, he made a joke about Lauryn Hill, who had just received a bunch of Grammy nominations. He played some of her music, then said, "And they wonder why we drag them behind trucks," a grotesque reference to James Byrd, a black man murdered in 1998 by being bound and dragged behind a truck.

The Greaseman was appropriately canned, then made the expected rounds of apologies. When that didn't work, he performed penance, working at a soup kitchen. According to his bio on Wikipedia, he enrolled in intensive therapy and counseling. He flogged himself in public. He licked sidewalks clean. When he would finally find work again as a DJ, the station owners would ultimately have to take back the offer, because of public disgust over Tracht's past. He disappeared into infomercials. But after a few years returned to radio—a changed man, of course.

So why was Tracht's career ruined, when other shock jocks and talk show hosts weather similar calamities? Howard Stern, Opie and Anthony, Marv Albert have all run into trouble, but they weren't ruined. That's because race wasn't part of the scandal. Opie and Anthony, after all, only insulted the Catholic Church. Generally, that's fair game. If the Catholics were really smart, they'd install a black transvestite pope. Pope RuPaul.

You're getting uncomfortable now, right? Thinking, "What the hell is Gutfeld doing defending this racist crap?" You're waiting for me to defuse this and make my point, right? Here it is: You look at examples like Richards and Tracht and you could reasonably conclude that racism is alive and well in America. You would be reasonably wrong. For I argue that those examples prove that, for the most part, racism—the kind of awful blatant racism you used to read about and see in movies—is fading. And the proof of that is in the aftermath of each incident.

Consider previous acts of racism—back when it was okay to be racist. The victims of racism truly were victims. They missed out on many freedoms we take for granted. Some lost their lives. Others had to play in a backup band for a horrible white singer.

But if you consider the victims in these contemporary cases, they were able to see the perpetrators dutifully and appropriately vilified. And erased from the public eye. Lauryn Hill probably has no memory of some jackass named the Greaseman. She might have been offended, but she's way bigger than some sad, unfunny sack of crap spouting bigoted baloney.

Comedian Tom Shillue said it perfectly after our third beer at a local tavern: "The only people hurt by racism these days are the racists." And thank God for that. ·

Even actual racists must crawl back under their rocks, knowing that if you express racism you are destroyed, never your target of derision. For this reason, I'm pretty sure there are very lucky kids these days who have no concept of racism, and aren't even aware of the debates raging all over cable and blogs. Maybe they'd know racism if it were in a video game somehow. Jim Crow for Xbox. But otherwise, they look at all of that and just shrug. Blatant, crappy racism seems like rotary phones or the American auto industry—something people way older than you might remember.

Waiting for me to break the tension? To stop with the uncomfortable "racism-is-in-decline" schtick? Okay, let me let you off the hook. Racism is wrong and evil. So there, I said it.

But I also say this: Racism as a source for outrage exists these days because it's a marvelous topic for talk shows, and it keeps Al Sharpton feeling relevant. Once Americans realize how outmoded this "racist culture" accusation is, Sharpton is out of work (of course, he can then rely on his vast array of skill sets to make a living).

But what about Janeane Garofalo? Making fun of her is old news, but she makes it so easy. She's a smart chick who once had a career but has now turned into something angry and shrill. She's transforming, like a slower version of Jeff Goldblum in *The Fly*. With tattoos, instead of the extra eyes.

I refer to an appearance she made on one of Keith Olbermann's failed shows that aired sometime in August 2011 (this was before he was fired by Current TV, which you can get if you have the dish—it's between the Hat Channel and the Sock Channel). When the topic of Herman Cain's quest for the presidency came up, she offered a theory: that he—a black man—was a plant, created by the Republican Party, to show that the party isn't full of racists. (If only they were that clever.) Cain was also created purely to paint a rosy picture of the Tea Party. Essentially, she was calling Cain an Uncle Tom. Remember, Cain is a successful black businessman who once captained Godfather's Pizza. He's also a rabid conservative, fiercely religious, and prone to speaking his mind, regardless of consequence. His targets are liberals, bloated government, and social programs that undermine individual responsibility. He is charming, outspoken, and in my view, sometimes wrong. But not as wrong as Janeane.

For her wacky conspiracy revealed her own repressive tolerance, which is nothing more than despicable racism: that a black man cannot truly think for himself and come to the conclusion that he's a conservative. As a lily-white liberal, she knew better about what black men think. We know she has no idea what blacks really believe. Research will show you that blacks are way more conservative than she could ever fathom. And how many more she's likely created, thanks to her misguided opinions!

And so, as a member of the tolerati who adheres to the tenets of liberal dogma, she can tolerate everything—except ideas that don't match her assumptions. Thus, a black man must be dehumanized, turned into an automaton programmed by rich white men, perhaps created in a right-wing lab by the evil genius Thomas Sowell.

On one TV show, I defended the poor misguided actress, saying that she was simply a Method actress, preparing for a role as a "bitter, narrow-minded idiot." But I was wrong. It wasn't a role. It was her liberal default mode set by the pernicious program of the politically correct, and an arrested development apparently spent trapped inside a Lisa Loeb song. She could no longer look at a highly successful black man and feel good about it. She had to tear Cain down. She had to ridicule him. She had to sap him of his value. She had to force the man to bow to her beliefs. She would only accept him as a worthy human being, if he agreed to disown his own conscience.

And here you have a really odd contrast. When Barack Obama ran for president, anyone who disagreed with his candidacy was usually labeled a racist. America, after all, is a racist country. Still, he won overwhelmingly—and he could only have won if a lot of white folks voted for him. But now he is president, and the accusations of racism still fly—even more frequently when he hits rocky political waters. Merely pointing out that the economy is getting worse under him—even if you voted for him a few years earlier—made you a bigot. How weird is it that we had another black presidential candidate and there is real racism afoot? Very weird. Emo Philips weird. I mean, Cain was insulted daily by those in the media because he's a black conservative. Mind you, they didn't go after him because he was conservative. They vilified him because he was conservative *and* black. He couldn't possibly, as a black man, have believed in individual freedoms, in working hard, in an entitlement-free culture. He had to be a plant. Worse than a plant. A pod. He had to be a hologram—a fictive black conservative hologram projected from a special lens implanted in Walt Disney's still-throbbing forehead!

If you think Garofalo is the worst culprit, you're wrong (to her dismay, I'm sure—she's very competitive). Witness D. L. Hughley, the black comedian and failed host of a short-lived CNN show. In a series of woefully unfunny tweets, he smeared Cain by saying that his face belongs "on a pancake box." For those of you under thirty, he was referring to Aunt Jemima. Yep, Cain was just an Uncle Tom, because he was a successful black man who didn't blindly follow the liberal assumptions that all black people are supposed to follow. And how should Cain respond to that? By saying D.L.'s face belongs under a hat that says GODFATHER'S PIZZA on it? You could just as easily use Garofalo's line about Cain on Hughley—that the attention he's received during his career is based on toeing the white liberal line.

Imagine if Nick DiPaolo, a conservative comedian, had tweeted that Obama's face belonged on a pancake box. He'd be on a boat to Cambodia faster than Michael Richards. But when Hughley tweeted that nonsense, the only people that noticed were a handful of conservative blogs. That's it. No one else raised an eyebrow. I relayed the tweet to Herman Cain, and he laughed. He expressed no sense of outrage or anger. It was beneath him. He just expected this kind of stuff, and thought it silly—and noted how mainstream liberals cannot accept a conservative black leader, for it destroys their comfy worldview. For if a black man rejects liberalism, he rejects all the do-good nonsense liberals believe in. They are no longer political sheep, and they see the consequences of white liberal guilt, which harms blacks more than a thousand unfunny comedians and DJs ever could.

On the topic of bad CNN shows, did anyone find it weird that Eliot Spitzer got a show, after what he had done with hookers? And with a face like something from Easter Island? It was perfectly acceptable, because his heart, if not his groin, was in the right place (where Spitzer's groin actually belongs, however, is something I'm not going to contemplate). Which is why he found another job, at Current TV. Repressive tolerance allows a pig to be a pig, and if it's at Current TV, at least the pig found adequate slop.

But in this day and age, you'd better know your place. And you better know it fast. Which leads me to Brett Ratner. There's no way around using that name without including the phrase "untalented schlub." Or if there is a way, it's a very long way around.

He committed the latest act of intolerance. He made a joke that was perceived to be "homophobic," even though his intention had nothing to do with attacking gays.

Back in the fall of 2011, this notorious nitwit was participating in a Q and A session after a screening of his flick *Tower Heist,* a piece of poop he had idiotically linked to the Occupy Wall Street phenomenon in an earlier interview. The plot—a heist caper—had a lot in sync with how people were feeling down at the protest sites, or something like that. Someone asked how the preparations for the upcoming Oscars (he was producing) were going, and he said, "Rehearsal is for fags."

Neither funny nor original, nonetheless it's a huge sin because it was deemed homophobic. Even though the dimmest of the dim could see it was just a knuckleheaded remark meant to convey "We're such badasses we don't need to rehearse." Or put another way, "The Oscars always suck, so why change now?"

After the predictable outcry from the supersensitive, Ratner announced he was stepping down as producer of the awards show. He did it in record time, actually, without bothering to put up the kind of fight you'd expect from the creative genius behind *Rush Hour* and *Rush Hour 2*. Apparently he had seen where these brouhahas usually end up, and—not as dumb as he looks—he could see he was on the losing end.

If it had only ended there with a simple, "I'm outta here." But

Ratner, a quick learner, realized that in order to clear himself, and save his name and career, he had to do the full penance, jumping on every sword he could find. So he didn't just say "I resign," he offered a long, pathetic letter of resignation to the academy. In the pantheon of shameless groveling, this would have won the Oscar . . . for shameless groveling.

Here's what he wrote, in part:

As difficult as the last few days have been for me, they cannot compare to the experience of any young man or woman who has been the target of offensive slurs or derogatory comments. And they pale in comparison to what any gay, lesbian, or transgender individual must deal with as they confront the many inequalities that continue to plague our world.

Having love in your heart doesn't count for much if what comes out of your mouth is ugly and bigoted. I will be taking real action over the coming weeks and months in an effort to do everything I can both professionally and personally to help stamp out the kind of thoughtless bigotry I've so foolishly perpetuated.

What a performance.

Ratner continued:

I am grateful to GLAAD for engaging me in a dialogue about what we can do together to increase awareness of the important and troubling issues this episode has raised and I look forward to working with them.

Note: Whenever you see the word *dialogue* in a political context, you are in the presence of pure, unadulterated bullshit of the liberal variety. This is a scientific axiom, which I just made up.

Now, I have no proof to back this up, but I don't believe Ratner wrote that letter. Also, the letter sucked. The suckiest part? Groveling to GLAAD. For saying "fags," a hurtful word if words do "hurt." Me, I would prefer a well-hurled epithet over a rock, crowbar, or empty wine bottle cracked over my head. But I realize that is not a fair comparison, and I apologize in advance. I will text you from Cambodia.

I said Ratner probably didn't write the letter, and I may be wrong. But all the catchphrases are in there, and I can't believe Ratner had that amazingly complex lexicon at the ready. Nope, he sat down with an expert in this malarkey and was told what to cut and paste. Either that, or Ratner went through the world's fastest brainwashing session ever. Or perhaps he secretly worked for GLAAD all along and had planned the whole thing. If so, I take back everything I said: the man's a genius.

Apparently, Ratner learned something in the last four or five years, other than how easy it is to sleep with B-list actresses. He knew the thing you gotta do, no matter what, is take the medicine, do the penance—even if the penance far outweighs whatever infraction you committed against the almighty tolerati.

For repressive tolerance, when violated, is the worst possible sin on the planet, and the penance must reflect that.

Two words must have echoed in Brett Ratner's cavernous but empty skull: Isaiah Washington. You remember him, no? He was the actor who once starred in that hit show lonely women and their cats watch, called *Grey's Anatomy*. He played the dreamy—I mean cocky—doctor Preston Burke.

Until he made a remark deemed outrageous by the Offense Police.

In October 2006, details emerged that Washington had called

his costar T. R. Knight a faggot, or something like that. Washington apologized for the words, especially since Knight had only recently come out of the closet. But the apology wasn't enough, because when you appear intolerant, you must *suffer*. You must lose something valuable, like your job. And yeah, Washington is black, which you'd think would offer him a little immunity, but in this day and age, gay trumps skin color, and he was going to suffer just like everyone else. Welcome to the tolerance sweepstakes, Mr. Washington. One wrong word and out you go.

Being interviewed on the red carpet at the Golden Globes, Washington joked that he wanted to be gay. "Please let me be gay," he implored, probably beginning to understand his place in this new universe. He then denied he ever called Knight a "faggot." But then Knight, in an appearance on *The Ellen DeGeneres Show,* said everyone heard him say it. So Washington apologized again, longer this time. Despite undergoing something called "executive counseling" (was it done at an airport Sheraton, with a free continental breakfast?), ABC announced the actor was dropped from the show.

So fast-forward five years and here I am at the gym, a few weeks or so after the Ratner controversy, and I look up at the TV in front of my stair-climber, and whom do I see? Mr. Washington, looking dapper with a beard and stylish glasses and a colorful shirt, appearing subdued yet relaxed, about to be interviewed by the delightful Fredricka Whitfield.

According to the CNN anchor:

It has been four years since actor Isaiah Washington starred in the hit television show *Grey's Anatomy* as the self-assured Dr. Preston Burke. That is, until he made an offensive remark back in 2007. In his book *A Man from Another Land,* Washington talks about life after *Grey's Anatomy,* the defeat, self-discovery, and his reawakening in West Africa. We talk face to face.

I guess Cambodia was too crowded with celebrities seeking "spiritual renewal."

And there you have it. The penance for an argument in which the word *faggot* was used was a pilgrimage to Africa—that lasted four years. Yep, four years. For one word, that's almost seven months per letter.

I'm sure what the actor did was ennobling—in the interview he talks about how he's already "saved lives." He said, "In fact, I have five hundred students in my school. That's what I've been doing for the last four years. And to get excited about saving real lives, that is the biggest adrenaline rush that I could have for someone like me."

And of course, none of this could have happened if it hadn't been for him getting canned from *Grey's Anatomy,* right, Fredricka?

> **WHITFIELD:** Had that experience at *Grey's Anatomy* not played out the way it did, would the inspiration to talk about this self-discovery or your mission and commitment to Sierra Leone have happened?
>
> **WASHINGTON:** Obviously, my exit from *Grey's* was a catalyst for sure. Even in loss you gain, even in loss you win, even in the "L" you get a "W."

No. What we got was a "B" and an "S."

And, there you go. From the utterance of one bad word, to self-imposed exile, to returning a changed man with a new book. Thank you repressive tolerance and cultivated outrage. Do you see the equation? The man says an offensive word and five hundred lives are saved. Hell, maybe *that's* a good thing.

These are phenomena so powerful they forced Washington to get in touch with his own victimhood—how he felt "Unattractive, all of it. Broad nose, full lips, the whole thing," from being a black man. And this guy's a handsome guy, for chrissake. If this guy had misgivings about his looks—Jesus Christ—then what hope do I have in this world? On a scale of one to ten, he's a thirteen! I must be hideous.

Anyway, this journey wasn't just about his own homophobia but also his own insecurity, his own pain (conveniently focused on racial characteristics, which was Washington hopefully floating a little victimhood of his own past the tolerati). And maybe now that story will erase the story that forced him to create this story. And he get can back to acting!

And so what Washington has just gone through is the path that awaits Ratner, and Ratner knows it.

Does it help? Who knows. It probably doesn't matter. Because the great thing about the whole cycle of Tolerance, Violation, and Penance is that there's always a new culprit, a new flub that surfaces and threatens to swallow a career because it has hurt the wrong feelings. Why? Because another special interest group emerges every couple of years. It used to be, legitimately, blacks. Currently, it's clearly gays. In a year or two, who knows? You'll recognize it the first time you hear a celebrity telling an interviewer how he or she was made to feel "inferior" growing up but has now "come to peace with who I am." "Comfortable in my own skin" is the modern go-to cliché. It could be dwarves (sorry, I mean little people). Or maybe very tall people (who now have support groups), or even Belgians. But it'll arrive, rest assured. And as soon as some gay celebrity says the word *midget* and then appears crying on *The View* before boarding a plane to Cambodia or Sierra Leone, you'll know we're onto a new cycle. (Note: As I edit this, Rosie O'Donnell is just getting stick for the very thing—ragging on little people. She apologized.)

But you don't even really have to hurt anyone's feelings—the perception that a comment might is all that it takes. Consider CNN's Roland Martin (wasn't he on *Laugh-In?*), whose tweets were deemed offensive to gays.

Martin was suspended by CNN after GLAAD complained about his tweets during the 2012 Super Bowl. In response to an underwear ad featuring six-pack meat bucket David Beckham, Martin tweeted:

AIN'T NO REAL BRUHS GOING TO H&M TO BUY SOME DAMN DAVID BECKHAM UNDERWEAR! #SUPERBOWL

He followed that with this charming missive:

IF A DUDE AT YOUR SUPER BOWL PARTY IS HYPED ABOUT DAVID BECKHAM'S H&M UNDERWEAR AD, SMACK THE ISH OUT OF HIM! #SUPERBOWL

As a middle-aged white guy, I don't know what "ish" is—I assume it's some sort of high-carb dip. At any rate, GLAAD tweeted to Martin that

ADVOCATES OF GAY BASHING HAVE NO PLACE AT @CNN

GLAAD smelled blood, and then issued a statement demanding Roland's removal from his network, citing the fact that he once referred to homosexuality as "sinful behavior." Martin claims he was only cracking on soccer—and by looking at the tacky tweets (and not being able to read his mind), we should probably take him at his word. It didn't matter. CNN threw Roland to the wolves, writing:

LANGUAGE THAT DEMEANS IS INCONSISTENT WITH THE VALUES AND CULTURE OF OUR ORGANIZATION, AND IS NOT TOLERATED. WE HAVE BEEN GIVING CAREFUL CONSIDERATION TO THIS MATTER, AND ROLAND WILL NOT BE APPEARING ON OUR AIR FOR THE TIME BEING.

So how did Roland react? Did he jump up and fight back, condemning both his network and GLAAD for a witch hunt based on innocent, albeit stupid and unfunny tweets? Nope, his job was more important than his spine. And so he quickly announced he would be meeting with GLAAD, even adding that he would look forward to "having a productive dialogue." There it is again—dialogue! Gutfeld's first scientific axiom.

God I hate dialogue. Especially productive dialogue.

But by granting GLAAD an interview, Martin validated their outrage—a pathetic response done solely to protect his career. I don't think it was a gay slur. But that doesn't matter. His response, in the face of mounting pressure, made it a gay slur. So what if the joke was about a soccer player, and that player has a great body, which apparently makes him a gay icon? Which doesn't follow. I mean, I have a great body. Godlike, really. Yet, I'm not a gay icon. Or if I am, nobody told me. I think they'd tell you, right?

Twitter seems to be rough turf these days for jokes, both good and bad. Remember the hysteria over the rise of Jeremy Lin, the undrafted fourth-stringer who scored at least 20 points in each of his first four games as a starter for the Knicks (this is lacrosse, right?). During that run, a sports columnist, Jason Whitlock, got a little too excited, tried too hard to be funny, tweeting this unfortunate but mildly humorous tweet:

SOME LUCKY LADY IN N-Y-C IS GONNA FEEL A COUPLE INCHES OF PAIN TONIGHT.

The joke, for those who don't follow, is a play on a stereotype that Asians have, on average, smaller penises than other ethnicities. Not surprisingly, this tweet set off the Asian American Journalists Association president, Doris Truong: "Outrage doesn't begin to describe the reaction of the Asian American Journalists Association to your unnecessary and demeaning tweet."

Okay, if outrage doesn't begin to describe the reaction, I wonder how Truong would feel about something that actually *hurt* someone—like a violent crime. I mean, she's talking about a stupid tweet, for God's sake—a tweet that probably never would have been noticed if it hadn't been for her knee-jerk, over-the-top response.

These are words, people. These are jokes. If that joke had been told at a comedy club, it would have garnered laughs—likely from the Asians in the crowd. That's the beauty of some racial humor—it's a test of how much you can take and how little really gets to you. Talk to anyone in the military, on a sports team, or on a police force—this sort of stuff is tame compared to the insults they fling at one another when drunk or sober. The fact that this is deemed beyond outrage shows you how wimpy our culture has become, and how we've let the purveyors of repressive tolerance clamp down on the conversation.

But in order to keep your job, you gotta bow to these forces of fragile feelings. And Whitlock did. Following the AAJA cry of outrage, he wrote his own "meh" culpa, asking for a little understanding: " . . . I then gave in to another part of my personality—my immature, sophomoric, comedic nature. It's been with me since birth, a gift from my mother and honed as a child listening to my godmother's Richard Pryor albums. I still want to be a stand-up comedian."

Yeah, me too. But that dream is about as likely to happen as my dream of being the first transgendered unicorn. And for God's sake, you think Richard Pryor would've apologized for this? It would likely have been the mildest thing he ever said.

But these incidents raise more sad questions about modern America. Are we becoming a nation of wusses if we let a silly tweet get to us? And isn't this more about the high we get from outrage, and the attention garnered when we cry foul? Could it be that Truong isn't really as outraged as she claims? Isn't that the real point—that repressive tolerance and fake outrage now mean every joke is an opportunity for attention, for sympathy, for justification of your organization? Are we really that friggin soft? You think Putin, or the Chinese, have noticed? (Yes.)

But come on, if you really feel outrage over that joke, how are you going to feel about a real issue? If we are to believe you are truly "beyond outrage," then this makes your real rage entirely meaningless.

And last, who is hurt by all this? Not Lin. Not Asians. Just Whitlock. But I guess that's the point. In the modern world of phony outrage and repressive intolerance, it's all about feeling important, and waiting for the next person to screw up so you can do it all over again. We've become a nation of scolds, slavering to rat out whoever we feel is next to step out of line. How long until children start calling a hotline to report their parents for "insensitive remarks" overheard at home? If and when that happens, I'm moving to Alaska, where they don't have phones.

I'M OKAY, YOU SHOULD DIE

IF YOU WANT TO SEE WHERE TOLERANCE STOPS and insanity begins, make fun of a celebrity on Twitter. Within minutes, the open-minded will erupt into outrage—the kind of response you'd expect from a mom watching a stranger slap her kid (which I've done on occasion). But of course these idiots don't even know the star, and the star—usually coked to the gills—wouldn't care if their fan lived or died. Yet the hopped-up outrage takes full bloom as if you've taken a hammer to a basket of kittens. Celebrities, after all, are America's mythological heroes—divine figures residing on Mount Olympus, behind the Hollywood sign, under the benevolent gaze of the Zeus-like George Clooney and Hera-like Barbra Streisand. And as we all know, you don't insult your god.

My favorite example of such tertiary outrage happened in August 2011, when Chris Brown, pop singer and chick-beater, tweeted about planking—the faddish practice of lying perfectly still on various surfaces, a pastime that could only catch hold in a very wealthy capitalist society suffused with self-irony (one suspects little planking in, say, Sudan). He wrote, and I paraphrase, that he'd love to be planking a beautiful woman. My friend Andy Levy responded in a tweet, "You spelled punching wrong."

Now, let me first say: Wow, do I wish I'd written that line.

In an instant Brown had sent his minions—angry and easily excitable fans known as Team Breezy—after Levy. For one solid night they graced Levy's Twitter feed with condemnations and threats, all spelled as only the current products of America's school system could manage.

The irony was rich: These were all women defending a man who brutally beat a woman (the hot pop star Rihanna, who has a crush on me, which is getting embarrassing) and sent her to the hospital.

The next night, after craploads of vicious tweets, Levy fashioned a delightful false apology, which he read on our late-night show, further inflaming the masses—by merely pointing out the fact that they were more upset about a joke than about violence against women.

The result? Death threats—the glorious Internet phenomenon of misguided, disproportioned outrage. The bulk of these dames were sad women, sitting at home tweeting support for a creep who doesn't give a damn about them.

Why the fake rage? Because it felt good. It felt good to get angry, and it felt good to target that anger at some late-night "Jew." Yep, you knew that would come up. Levy's a Jew, which wasn't lost on the outraged. What would they have done if they saw him on the street? Because manufactured outrage usually lives, then dies, on the Web—probably nothing.

But you never know.

And wishing death isn't limited to groupies—even stars get into the act. Take Green Day's Billy Joe Armstrong, a big star and a little person—in every sense—who, in front of thousands of fans at a concert in Lima, screamed that he couldn't wait for Steve Jobs to die of "fucking cancer." There was a video of it up on YouTube, but it's since been removed. A year after saying that, Armstrong got his wish, and Jobs died of cancer at the age of fifty-six. There wasn't a lot of press coverage on what this whiny troll spewed. There's a reason for that. It's A-OK.

First, let's point out that Green Day is an especially left-wing band, which condemns evil corporations and the mindless automatons who work for them. So they're okay. They reflect the Occupy Wall Street mentality that anything that makes a profit while wearing a tie (as opposed to a nose ring) must be evil. But how funny is it that Warner Bros. has removed the video from YouTube, in order to protect their product (because that's what you are, Armstrong: a product). At this point, Armstrong should thank his lucky tattoos he isn't eking out a living at the Shoe Tree.

And last time I checked, you can buy Green Day albums on iTunes, the brainchild of the man he wished dead. The bigger point: in the current climate of repressive tolerance, you can wish people dead—if they are the right people to wish dead and you're the right person doing the wishing.

When Heath Ledger died, Bill Maher's thoughtful comment was wishing that it had been Rush Limbaugh instead. He did this on his show, *Real Time,* and it bummed me out that no one on the panel actually said anything remotely critical of it. I'd like to think, if I had been there, I would have smacked him in his marsupial-like face. But I was told, as a child, never to fight people with marsupial-like faces. The saliva is infectious.

The fact is, when someone on the right says something that stupid, he or she will meet universal criticism. From both sides. When a comedian on my show remarked that he wanted a low-rent bimbo celebrity placed on Obama's terrorist kill list, I told him that was wrong. It's ugly and stupid—and risky. There are too many crazies out there convinced TV hosts are sending them telepathic instructions. For the record, I've only ever beamed one directive: to go out and buy this book. (Glad to see you're pay-ing attention. Stay tuned for further instructions concerning back rubs.) If you're going to be intolerant of that kind of thing when it's said about people you like, you gotta do the same for those you don't.

The left isn't so consistent. You can wish death or ill will on anyone from George Bush to Sarah Palin, and you'll probably get a grin from every liberal blogger, comic, and talking head. But say anything like that about a precious liberal icon and you will be run out of town. See Hank Williams, Jr., who compared Obama to Hitler. ESPN promptly dropped him from the intro of *Monday Night Football,* a decision I get—they're a private company, and if they want to fire someone who might harm their brand, they have every right to do it. It's not a freedom-of-speech issue: Williams has every right to say whatever he wants. He won't get arrested for it. But he certainly can get fired for it. Funny, though, how ESPN re-acts differently when the targets aren't liberal. When Mike Tyson made those lewd comments about Sarah Palin on ESPN, the hosts laughed uproariously. Maybe they were laughing at Mike's facial tattoo, which I'm not sure he realizes is there. And when Kenny Mayne tweeted about how he almost rammed a car because it had a Palin bumper sticker on it, the media response was translated as "we feel the same way."

Wishing death on anyone is, in my risky opinion, sucky (unless they screw up your drink order). Especially since you'll get that wish, at some point. But what if you make a list of people you want to kill, some on the list being Americans—and you actually mean to kill those people? And then you actually *do* kill those people? The media response would be in unison: Impeach Bush! But what if it wasn't Bush who made that list? What if it was Obama? Well, the universal disgust is strangely muted. Aside from a very few consistent minds, you didn't hear much from the left about the Obama kill list, which led to the welcomed drone-death of Anwar al-Awlaki. Tolerance for the murder of American citizens seems unimaginable under Bush, but totally acceptable for Obama.

That's the beauty of Obama—he is impervious to accusations of brutality because he was the choice of the tolerati. Which allows him to kill at will (and avoid interrogating live people). The man has killed craploads of crappy people. He got Osama, and countless scumbags who work for him. It's something I love about Obama, and it's why I love anyone who helped him in the effort to crush these cockroaches—which includes Bush. (But not Eric Holder, who's been too busy giving free guns to the Mexicans. No wonder we have a trade deficit!)

And this illustrates an interesting phenomenon about liberalism: Sometimes liberals can be just as deadly as the most warlike hawk and get away with it—because they're liberal. If you're the most progressive president we've ever seen, the tolerant masses will tolerate you pulling shit off they'd never let Bushcheneyhitler get away with. It's a brilliant bit of sleight of hand, perfected in Hollywood by the likes of Maher and those twin sweathogs the Weinstein brothers, who may be the most unlikely lotharios since Chang and Eng.

I'm not knocking Obama. I'm absolutely for the kill list, and for wishing these people dead (I'd even add a few names to it, like Ahmadinejad and my editor). But I'd be for it if it was Bush doing the same thing. That makes me different from the left. For them, you can vaporize your enemies as long as you give us a little soaring rhetoric and a heartfelt autobiography or three. It's a simple trade-off. I guess it's a good thing Obama doesn't write poetry. He might bomb Cuba.

UNREAL ESTATE

WHEN FINANCE IS TRUMPED BY FEELINGS, we are all screwed. According to some recent statistics, home ownership has had its biggest drop since the Great Depression, down to 65.1 percent. Forty-one states declined in home ownership since 2000, and it's worse for blacks: home ownership fell to 44.3 percent. Whites are now 1.63 times more likely to own a home than blacks. (That's it for my statistics. They were never my strong point. I actually fell asleep while pulling those numbers off a blog.)

How did that happen? How did we get to this horrible place, where tracts of homes lie vacant, overgrown with weeds, populated by bugs and mice—and in some areas of Florida, alligators and senior citizens?

Well, obviously the financial crisis, triggered largely by the massive housing bubble bursting, didn't help. Sure, there's high unemployment too, but how did so many people suddenly default on so many loans?

Because they shouldn't have received them to begin with.

People blame the banks and Wall Street for bundling high-risk loans and selling them like poisoned pancakes, but those loans had to be approved for a reason. And the reason, was . . . wait for it . . . *tolerance!*

Right now Fannie May and Freddie Mac have all but stopped

encouraging loans to high-risk individuals. This is all but an admission that their earlier practices were what caused this mess. It's like when I stop ordering takeout from the same place after three solid days of diarrhea. I see the link and make the correction.

Those lending practices—making it really easy for high-risk borrowers to buy homes they couldn't afford—arose from a fear of looking mean and heartless. Seeing a large group of people as a class who need government help, politicians realized they couldn't simply redistribute wealth—that wouldn't fly with you and me. So the alternative was redistribution through low-interest-rate loans, getting them on that first rung of the fabled property ladder. Even if it meant that the rung would give way and send the whole thing crashing down.

The banks were encouraged to approve the loans, and for a while everyone was happy, or at least not in foreclosure. But what would happen if some banking dude had said that this practice might be a bad idea: that approving loans to millions of people who can't afford them spells disaster? That would be discriminatory. Clearly, Mr. Evil Banker (who must look like the mustachioed Monopoly guy) doesn't want blacks or Hispanics to own homes. Yep, if you don't approve of that loan, you're probably a racist, Mr. Moneybags (never mind that whites got nailed, too). This implication removed the sole purpose of a bank: to be the shrewd bad guy when it comes to doling out the money (sort of how my wife sees me). Remember, in old movies, bankers were always denying loans. The poor farmer would trek miles to the city bank, only to be told there is no third mortgage for his roof. Now, gleefully, those vile creatures in suits could be the good guy, handing out homes like they were those tiny red plastic pieces from a Monopoly game.

This is not to absolve the greedy folks who bundled the loans and sold them—they simply added the whipped cream to this dessert of financial ruin. But imagine how hard it might have been to say no to the process in the beginning, since the process was for the "greater good." Getting poor people on the property ladder is a nice gesture, as is knitting a "peace quilt"—although that doesn't mean world peace suddenly breaks out. But it's inherently destructive if they can't stay there. It was affirmative action using private property, and over time, those who can't afford to stay on that rung can only do one thing: jump off. If only someone other than Republicans had had the balls to risk the shrieks of "racism" and "intolerance" to point this out, perhaps we'd be in a better place. One with a roof over our heads that the bank isn't about to repossess.

The banks and the government weren't the only guilty parties. Those who bought the homes had a hand in this mess. A friend I'll call Sven was a highflying executive who spent most of his money on girls, booze, and trips. How the hell he got a loan to buy a condo, with little money in the bank, was beyond me—and him. When his interest rates went crazy, he short sold that property.

We may end up paying for Sven's default. My other friend (I have two, I swear), a freelance designer who never made much money, was able to purchase a sizable house in an outer burb in California. When it became painfully clear that designing business cards was not the booming industry "Ryan" thought it would be (who needs business cards when everyone is out of business?), he saw a lawyer, who advised him to stop making mortgage payments (but be sure to keep paying him, of course!). Oddly, he was still able to afford a lavish wedding. So why did he choose to pay for that and not put the money into that house? Because he didn't have to. Buying that house as a high risk made the choice less substantial. "I guess it wasn't meant to be," he said, and he returned to renting, with seven years of bad credit ahead. Thanks to the friendly bankers, an enabling government, and an ideology that puts tolerance ahead of common sense, he just took the path of least resistance At least he has those wedding pictures. Everybody in America should get a copy. After all, we paid for them.

Meanwhile, it's idiots like me who are stuck paying the bill. I can't remember missing a mortgage payment, and I cannot even get refinancing. I am a maker, who is getting taken. But in this backwards equation, I'm not a victim, so I get punished. I would like to buy a bigger place and move, but the down payments required since the meltdown are so huge that I am stuck in an apartment slightly larger than your local Starbucks. Not that I'm complaining. I am a tiny person, so simply by proportion my shoebox of an apartment is actually a mansion. Bigger if you count the ventilated storage container installed under the living room.

POOP STARS

I GUESS THEY WERE THE PEOPLE we were waiting for. Nancy Pelosi called their actions "spontaneous." President Obama could empathize with their "frustrations." Celebrities like Alec Baldwin, Susan Sarandon, and yes, even Penn Badgley (of *Gossip Girl,* and the name of my pet hamster) expressed solidarity with those participating in the occupation of Wall Street.

The ragged movement began, as many pointless things do, on Facebook, where some activists (part of an anarchist Canadian group called Adbusters) announced their intentions to camp out in a park in the heart of the financial district. What made it fun and interesting was their lack of focus. They had no principles, so they offered a poll to choose what to protest. In sum, they had no idea what they were protesting, they only knew that protesting would feel really good. What this illustrated, really, was that it's hard to protest when you've already gotten what you wanted: a very liberal president, one who reengineered health care so even the most bedraggled can get treated for "hackey sack ankle." They weren't actually going to speak truth to the man, because, really, they were on the same side as the man. They were liberals, and liberals were in power.

Contrary to Nancy Pelosi, this was not a spontaneous gathering, for among these sign-carriers were the same old silly souls—anarchists from the WTO days, Code Pink from the antiwar protests, and assorted middle-aged hippies who found out that wearing a Guy Fawkes mask might look really cool with a gray ponytail.

What struck me about this movement was how the media embraced it like an adorable kitten. It was a striking departure from their mocking dismissal of the Tea Partiers.

Remember, the Tea Party were old people in tricorn hats, spouting phrases they picked up from Glenn Beck, all virulent Obama-haters, whose distaste for him was obviously due to his skin color, not his policies. Sure, they talked about the perils of government spending more than it takes in, but that was just code for "we hate black people." One network, which rhymes with MSNBC, showed footage of a Tea Partier strapped with a gun—filming and editing it in a manner to obscure the fact that he was black (which would have killed the "angry white male" story line). Comedians everywhere embraced the OWS movement, because it beat wondering if the waitress at the Des Moines "Chuckle House" had an STD.

The people who ridiculed the Tea Party now felt, in their hearts and heads, that OWS was the "real" protest movement—one that morphed into an attack on corporations and banks and anyone with money. They were the enemy: people who made money. They weren't necessarily in power, but it didn't matter. It was a call for class warfare, and it erupted with hundreds of arrests on the Brooklyn Bridge. These arrests were no surprise.

As they would surely be recorded, instantly romanticizing the movement—giving it more momentum as it demonized the police, who had better things to do. No cop really wants to wrestle or

Mace a snotty protester, because even he or she knows it won't win sympathy on YouTube. But it's their job, and they have to do it—knowing full well the second reason for an activist to get arrested is to unleash legal warfare. Just days after the arrests, the lawsuits began.

And another reason for the arrests: so a twenty-four-year-old unemployed doofus can, in twenty years, brag that he was "there," fighting the man. Even if he still isn't sure who "the man" is. Still, he could paint himself as a revolutionary. It might get him laid at a poetry reading. Hopefully, one of mine. My haiku chops are really evolving.

During all this, I was reluctant to fall into stereotyping the rabble, for that made me no better than the jerks who did the same to the Tea Partiers.

My reluctance lasted two hours, for their behavior made restraint impossible. From the very beginning they embraced the stereotype: groups of drum-playing men leaving trash and filth everywhere, shrill protesters screaming at children—and the perfect symbol of the protest itself: a man defecating on a police car. That was their "Kent State."

The First Amendment is delightful. Vital. In many ways, it's what really separates us from other developed democracies like Vermont. But this romanticization of protest for protest's sake has really got to stop. The act itself isn't enough—you're supposed to actually have a point. But to the media, the process is a romantic end unto itself. As long as you're "raising awareness," you're a hero. If you're cutting school, blocking traffic, and channeling rage, you're participating "in the process" and "making your voice heard." That's the problem—we have too many friggin voices making themselves heard. I have enough voices in my head already, thank you.

You know one of the real reasons we got OWS? Because there are no more decent rock festivals. Trust me, they're the same.

Funny how the media wanted this new phenomenon to be *their* Tea Party (after all, the Coffee Party failed miserably). So let's compare the two movements. It'll be worth it, trust me.

During the Tea Party, they actually got permits, not parasites. Yep, they organized orderly and calmly—and with a few odd exceptions, seemed affable. With lawn chairs, fanny packs, visors, and flags, it was like a yearlong Fourth of July picnic, minus the fistfights between cousins. Yeah, it was corny, but it was also calm.

As far as I could tell, there were few arrests made during the Tea Party events. At the Brooklyn Bridge rally alone, there were between six hundred and seven hundred. Probably the worst thing that happened at a Tea Party rally was a grass stain on Marge's diaper bag. Or a really unfortunate singalong featuring a greeter from Walmart dressed as a Founding Father.

The cleanup after a Tea Party rally was minimal. Yep, they took their lawn chairs home and picked up after themselves—they didn't leave stained mattresses and filthy cardboard rafts in the street. The Occupiers were different, leaving a mess for everyone else to clean up. I guess they were giving it to the man—if the man picked up garbage for a living. Here they were, "occupying" Zuccotti Park, getting catered food shipped in, and complaining about their foam mattresses. I know a few hundred thousand fellow occupiers who would kill for those conditions. But they're occupying Afghanistan at present.

During the Tea Parties, there were no riot police, no nudity, no shirtless bums using a business's bathrooms without paying for even a cup of coffee. No property was damaged, no traffic was blocked, no lives were disturbed, no attempt was made to lure the police to commit an "atrocity" to be uploaded on YouTube.

Meanwhile, a cop who Maced a protester at a Wall Street rally had his personal info released on the Web, and haters were encouraged to harass him and his family. And because every "occupation" culminated in a disgusting mess, the surrounding businesses that were initially sympathetic with them turned sour. These people sucked, they concluded.

Which leads me to a bigger distinction: the Tea Partiers were united by a few central singular principles: a return to limited government, personal responsibility, and creamier macaroni salads (other than obsessive Atkins dieters, who can argue with these things?). There were no uniting principles for the OWS. So it became a grab bag of the same old progressive platitudes—railing against everything from corrupt banks, to the death penalty, to degradation of the environment (which did not stop them from littering). The only thing they refused to condemn was their own boorish, dangerous, and deviant behavior. And there were loads of examples. The only thing thicker than the OWS rap sheet was the health care bill. When the tourists showed up, it was like a commie theme park.

Which makes the media response so beguiling. Their tolerance for the shrill and bedraggled Wall Streeters seemed boundless; their mockery for the more peaceful Tea Partiers equally endless. Why is that? Because their naive romanticism, tied to their own failed dreams, made it so. The media loved OWS because it's easy to love and tolerate those you secretly want to be.

President Obama endorsed the sentiment of the OWS protesters because they were no different from him when he was a college kid, and later a community organizer. In his twenties and thirties, he would have been there, locking arms, sitting on the grass, perhaps in a cool fedora, a cig dangling from his lips (a frightened dog nearby).

Still, I tolerate both movements—they are equally valuable, for different reasons. The Tea Party was a peaceful plea for some kind of correction: let's spend less and avoid turning into another piss-poor European country. The Wall Street protest illustrated the mess that is our education system. None of these angry agitators knew how an economy works. They railed against corporations, while wearing Nikes. They bemoaned the billions made by Apple, while pecking their manifestos on iPads. (It should be noted that "pecking" a manifesto significantly diminishes its impact.) But by tolerating them, and shining a light on them, we will hopefully teach a lesson to rest of America: it is better to make something than try to take something. And a college education is worth about as much today as a driftwood sculpture made by a Santa Cruz hippie.

Still, the second weekend of October 2011 was a great one for people bearing rattails, crappy tattoos, and head lice. Yep, the owners of Zuccotti Park—where the protesters were camping—caved. This happened, according to Mayor Bloomberg, after some New York pols made "threatening" calls to the property company, vowing to make their lives difficult if they evicted the unsavory mass of angry chanters.

So thanks to repressive tolerance, the park owner must do nothing about those camping on *his* property; instead he must let them do so, or he will appear intolerant. Intolerance is a public relations nightmare, so it's best to huddle back in your rich man's cave and pray for snow.

Which is essentially what the city did. The city, so far, at that point, had done little more than grouse quietly. And so the defiant protesters, sensing blood in the water, dug in even more, and the much-needed cleanup was delayed, as local business owners took the hit (especially their bathrooms). The hippie sleepover continued, rife with drugs, bongo-playing, naive late-night blathering, and assaults. Feeling emboldened from their recent victory, they later marched up Seventh Avenue, to protest on a pleasant Saturday in the middle of Times Square.

I watched a video of a young, comely protester explaining why she was there. "Imagine," she said, "how much better the world would be if there was no money." Of course, I have no idea how she paid for her education (my guess is, at some point, we will). You think she'll still be dreaming of a world without money when she's single and leaning on forty? The first capitalist pig with decent benefits will have her saying "I do" before you can say, "Jane Fonda, meet Ted Turner."

In the interest of tolerance, the media has no choice but to encourage the myth that all protesters are victims—by overlooking the protesters' own lily-white affluence, their expensive undergrad and graduate degrees, their trust funds, their iPads, their iPods, and so on.

One must also dismiss or obscure elements of the protest that would sicken 99 percent of Americans. Watching CNN, I caught them describing some crazy protest in Rome, as an expression of solidarity with the stuff going on here in the States. They referred to the unsavory violence (car fires, mainly) as performed by anarchists who had "infiltrated" the protests. But as far as I can tell, *infiltrated* is not an adequate synonym for *organized*. Because if you look at any or all of the protests, many of their mouthpieces call themselves anarchists. And the folks that started the OWS protests—the Canadian outfit Adbusters—are proud anarchists.

It's not uncommon to find, among the young, an easy condemnation of capitalism and money. When you're seventeen, saying "Money is the root of all evil," especially when accompanied by a hit off a bong—well, it sounds so romantic. It isn't until you grow up that you find that evil is the root of all evil, and money makes life good. And if you haven't realized that as an adult, you generally either have made no money or you have too much of it. See George Soros.

This is the laziest and dumbest kind of repressive tolerance: a hatred of corporations and people who work within them. I've not done years of research on the idea of a corporation, but I get what it is—and I want to explain it as simply as possible so the next time your tattooed nephew returns from Cornell to lecture you on corporate greed, you can slice and dice him like an egg in a Slap Chop.

The simplest definition of a corporation is that it is a group of people performing an activity that one person cannot do alone. In return for this activity, they get money. The money then goes to the people in the corporation to provide for their families, the largest sum going to those who started the whole damn thing and generally took the most risk at some point.

Now, what's the difference between a corporation and a protest? They are similar: both are organized activities performed by a group of individuals. And they both make things. One makes a product that enriches your life. The other makes a scene, and a traffic mess.

One makes money. The other makes noise. So yeah, they are the same—except one really sucks.

Is making money bad? Would the world be a better place without money, as the young lass hoped (she was so cute—like a puppy explaining brain surgery). Well, without money, we would have to trade for stuff, a solution some protesters put forth as a replacement for our present system. If I wanted a glass of milk, I suppose

I could offer you my hat. But you don't need a hat. You need to pay for your daughter's braces. I could give you my belt for that milk, but then my pants would fall down. And you still wouldn't be able to pay for your daughter's braces (plus, you'd be awestruck). If only there were a symbol of worth—a currency, if you will—that someone could use in exchange for product, that he could save and then spend on something he really needs! It would be so much simpler!

For fun, the next time you have a discussion with your anti-capitalist nephew, offer to "buy" his Che Guevara T-shirt. In exchange, offer something he would not find the least bit appealing (this book, for example). Then after a series of nos, finally offer him a hundred dollars. He will take it. He can now buy another Che shirt, an MP3 of the new Tom Morello acoustic set, and perhaps a veggie, gluten-free burrito. Meanwhile, you can go into the yard and burn the shirt in front of him. That's the only way to make that shirt worth a hundred dollars.

Repressive tolerance isn't the only problem. We actually put up with protests because we're an easygoing nation. People reacted to the protesters not with anger but with curiosity. People took pictures. Tourists took pictures of people taking pictures. To them, a protester was like that guy or gal in silver paint who looks like the Statue of Liberty. But with a nose ring. They're scragglier versions of the Naked Cowboy. People gave them money the same way you'd toss coins to a street juggler. They were emblems of a big city that tourists find quirky and neat. But after ten minutes, visitors from Iowa would get bored by the chanting, or unnerved by the unstable men eyeing their daughters or sons, and depart quickly to buy a 50-pound drum of chocolate at the M & M store.

The media, however, continued to indulge the dippy drama,

including all that whining about college debt. Sorry, they made that choice. By the time you're twenty, you should know that a degree in Peace Studies is not going to feed the cat. It likely means, at some point, you'll have to eat the cat (marinate it first—trust me).

So what happens when you indulge a tantrum? The answer is always: more tantrums. In the British riots over the summer, the criminals beating the crap out of people got away with it because lefty scribes identified their actions as part of a greater struggle—against greed, corporatism, capitalism, racism, and royalism. But everyone actually participating knew: the riots weren't about rage but about looting and maybe some groping.

This isn't the first time the media has done this. Remember how the Rodney King riots seemed justified—when in reality it was people stealing electronics and burning down strip malls. Through the prism of repressive tolerance, the next step is a paralyzing guilt that permits all kinds of behavior. And it's behavior directed at those who work hard for a living: shopkeepers, deli owners, small businesses that keep a community alive.

So why do people who work always end up being the bad guy? I mean, it's the person who never works who's the jerk. In your own life, there's always one lazy dope who lives off everyone else. We see this person as a loser. And the person who brings home the bread is, well, the breadwinner. That's how life works. It's in our DNA to despise dirtbags who want to get over on the rest of us. It goes all the way back. There was always one caveman who faked an injury, then suddenly jumped up when his buddies returned with the armful of berries. The difference is, he wasn't a hero because he spent the day lying around doodling in the dirt. He was the moocher. And, quite rightly, he was generally fed to a mastodon.

But out of some sense of liberal guilt, the media, and the entertainment industry, in particular, have reversed the belief. They romanticize the shiftless and demonize the wealthy and industrious. If you look at most movies these days, the villains don't wear black hats—they carry BlackBerrys. A briefcase in a movie is short for "soulless corporate ghoul."

Edward Jay Epstein nailed this in a *Wall Street Journal* piece called "The Corporate Exec: Hollywood Demon." There he listed a number of examples where Hollywood repeatedly casts moneymakers as the bad guys of society. In *Syriana,* the villain was Big Oil. In the remake of *The Manchurian Candidate,* the original Soviet Union villain was replaced by an American company "loosely modeled on the Halliburton Corporation."

Ahh . . . evil Halliburton. A shibboleth that could gain you entrance into Arianna Huffington's blogs or cocktail parties. But if you asked anyone what Halliburton really does, they'd probably tell you it doesn't matter, because they are evil. (I think they make fish sticks or something.)

Epstein notes that Jonathan Demme, in his DVD commentary that accompanies the *Manchurian* remake, admits to copping out when choosing the villain. He avoided making Saddam Hussein's forces the bad guys because he didn't want to "negatively stereotype" Muslims. I'd call Demme an "idiot," but I don't want to stereotype "idiots."

Never mind that this is insulting to Muslims (Demme must assume all Muslims see themselves in Hussein's henchmen).

Trying to avoid appearing intolerant pretzels you beyond physical possibility. Let me quote Epstein's piece, about Demme's film:

Not only was neither Saddam Hussein nor Iraq mentioned in a film about the Iraq-Kuwait war, but the Manchurian corporation's technicians rewire the brains of abducted U.S. soldiers with false memories of al Qaeda–type jihadists so that they will lay the blame for terrorist acts committed by American businessmen on an innocent Muslim jihadist.

Good lord. So in real life we have terrorist acts, which are committed by terrorists. But get this: In Hollywood, that's idiotic. Yep, perhaps we were all brainwashed into thinking terrorists are Islamic! Remember, in New York, that beautiful September morning, when planes flew into those buildings? *Ha!* That *never* happened. Well, at least the way you saw it. Through collective brainwashing, the entire country was made to believe that it was al Qaeda when in fact Dick Cheney was operating those planes from an underwater volcano sea lab made of human skulls. I'll bet he had a calico cat in his lap as he did it.

There, I just created, in five minutes, a treatment for Demme's next film. I expect a producer's credit, and a cameo as an angry dwarf.

So why are corporations the perfect villain for movies? They don't complain. If you make a gay villain, GLAAD will write seventy versions of the same nasty letter and then picket your children's piano recital. Remember *The Sopranos,* and all the guff they got for making mobsters Italian? (What the hell else would they be, Swedish?) Something tells me corporations like Halliburton don't employ representatives who review scripts with the studios. It's not that they don't have better things to do (which they do). They realize no one will listen.

But there's a root issue here: the evil corporations are really a stand-in for hatred of America. As Calvin Coolidge once said, "The chief business of America is business." But for Hollywood, we've just been too good at it. How dare we devise the best political and economic system in history! Don't you know the disparities that creates with Marxist collectives struggling for a neutral carbon footprint?

And, once again, "America" for most of these people is really a stand-in for "Daddy." Who was successful, made money, and sent me to an expensive liberal arts college.

So what's the endgame for proponents of repressive tolerance when it comes to OWS? My guess is, unless they were hard-core anarchists of the Adbusters variety, they might not have one. But it does give us the sense of a world where everything is permitted, and no one dares to question the damage caused by those who seek to destroy rather than create.

More to the point: What happens when Mommy and Daddy no longer care if junior shits in his pants?

You get a lot of shit, at least in Los Angeles.

As the weather grew colder, the cops knew it was time to strike— as even the most liberal mayors were starting to regret cozying up to anarchists and drifters. Which is what was happening in Los Angeles, at the start of December 2011, where sanitation officials started hauling away 30 tons of debris from the Occupy L.A. encampment—not including the protesters.

Now, 30 tons is a lot of trash. To give you an idea of the mass of that, I did some calculations. Then I lost them at a bar.

But if all you see is heaps of garbage, then you're missing two bigger points. The first is an old one: No one cares about things they don't own. To quote the great Milton Friedman, "When everybody owns something, nobody owns it, and nobody has a direct interest in maintaining or improving its condition."

Milt was a smart guy, and that one sentence succinctly explains why you would never poop in your driveway, but a protester will.

The second point is less philosophical but more relevant to this book. Why was the trash left, and why did the city have to pick it up? Why weren't the protesters forced to clean it up?

Because that would have been mean. The L.A. mayor had already expressed allegiance with these fighters of injustice, and he was willing to have the city absorb the cost of cleaning up their messes—rather than risk appearing intolerant of a group of folks the media had already deemed saintly.

Worse, after a monumental mess was made, do you know who the victims are? Yes, still the protesters. According to the *L.A. Times,* in a piece filed on December 3, 2011, despite many of the three hundred protesters being released from jail after only a few days, the writer explains, struggles lie ahead for these aggrieved souls. One of the movement leaders suggested the protesters may actually need therapy. Several protesters claimed that they were forced to urinate in bags while being taken to various jails (funny that this evacuation was probably little different from what they were doing at the camp, but if it was, it was more sanitary than whizzing against tents). Add to the trauma being forced to endure hours wearing plastic handcuffs and you can see why the media believes they are today's Freedom Riders. My God, even I feel traumatized having to write about their trauma. Perhaps you are now feeling equally traumatized reading my own traumatic words about their trauma. Perhaps I am guilty of creating a trauma daisy chain! Does Obamacare cover post-Occupy stress disorder? This nation is desperately short of occupational therapists!

On one show back in 2012 I said that OWS would likely be a "make or break" moment for Obama, our most tolerant president. How can our man—who totally "got" the movement—now reject calls for revolution?

But then I remember, a few years back, him saying to bank CEOs, "Be careful. My administration is the only thing standing between you and the pitchforks."

Well, now it appears like he's not only gotten out of the way, but through the use of the language of class warfare (constantly repeating "fair share" and ragging on the successful), is acting as their head cheerleader. When you consider what OWS has come to represent: the rapes, the assaults, the attacks on police, the sexually transmitted disease outbreaks, the widespread vandalism, the Cleveland bridge bomb plot—and an attack planned on his own campaign office in Chicago—someone should tell him he backed the wrong team.

STALIN GRADS

FOR SOME REASON, ADULTS CAN ONLY address two political alternatives. Left and right. Liberal, conservative. Democratic, Republican. Unicorn, gryphon. Colin Quinn aptly pointed out that our American system has only one more option than the USSR had during their brutal days (days gleefully endorsed by the *New York Times*'s Walter Duranty, earning him a Pulitzer and Stalin's enduring affection—but more on that later). Fact is, that extra option means *everything*—it's what separates us from Berkeley. But what does it say about us that we let this narrow, binary thinking cloud our ability to discern what's funny and what's offensive?

My feeling is, nothing is offensive . . . until it's not funny. Then it's lame. Making a pedophile joke isn't offensive. But going up to the mother of a victim and telling one is lame. So a hint: Don't do that. It's bad form.

But it's all about what side of the duopoly (a word I stole from *Reason*'s Nick Gillespie, along with his iPhone) you're on. If you're a conservative, you will laugh at what Dennis Miller says and scowl when you read a tweet by Alec Baldwin. If you're a liberal, you'll scream with fits of laughter over a Bill Maher gibe but then announce, solemnly, as if you're a comedic historian, "Dennis

Miller just isn't funny since he found conservatism." You'll get pissed off if someone you really like deviates from the assumptions you assume you once shared with them.

There is an in-between area in there, somewhere. It's a little place I like to call "In-Betweenville." Righties who think Baldwin is a troubled mind but a great comedic actor (me), and lefties who get the weirdness of the stuff I do (comedians like Pete Dominick and Greg Proops). But In-Betweenville is overwhelmed by the other two sides.

Are both sides equal in the sins of fake outrage, launching darts of repressive intolerance? Or is one guiltier than the other? Yes, I'm leaving In-Betweenville, to criticize the left.

I say this only because the left have been great at churning outrage for a far longer time, and without impediment. In a few years, the right may be just as obnoxious and humorless as the left (I hope not). But for now, the left are the New York Yankees of repressive tolerance and manufactured outrage—the right are the Bad News Bears.

But I need to ask myself: When I get mad, do I get mad because something really bugs me? Or do I just hate the people getting me mad? Because outrage-wise, I've been to Barney Frank and MSNBC. But I've never been to me.

Let's once more compare the Tea Party and the Occupiers. I count as friends people involved in both groups. I favor one over the other. I admit to mocking the Occupiers in a simplistic fashion, but the mockery comes from real concerns I have about their methods. I can also admit that the way people ridicule the Tea Party over being old and racist, I label the Occupiers as dirty and naive. No doubt, philosophically, I have more in common with the Tea Party. I'm a small-government kinda guy. And I admire and love many of these newbies, and it took a lot to get them out of that Barcalounger.

Their adversaries conclude that the Tea Party's anger is racist in origin. This, in my opinion, is a vicious smear. The origin of their anger is, well, anger! People get "fed up" when they feel cheated, or their future threatened. But calling them racist is what you'd do if you just can't stand them, period. It's shorthand for "I don't need to talk to you."

For the left and the mainstream media, these people protesting at the health care town halls were idiots. For those on the right, they were legitimately speaking truth to power. For me? I hate confrontation. I hate shouting. I get uncomfortable around this sort of thing. It's why I can't go to the DMV. And so I have two cars and no driver's license. (I'm not kidding.)

But when I saw the liberal media ripping these people, I sensed unfairness. The Tea Partiers are older. And unhip. These were polyester protesters and getting mocked because of that. That's funny for the first ten minutes, but lazy and boring for the rest.

This kind of ageism (and I hate myself already for using that term) blanketed the criticism against the Tea Party movement. The fact that their events were clean and well behaved made them corny and dorky. What do you expect from people with AARP cards in their wallets and Winnebagos in their driveway?

But these were the "benign" insults. The stuff got way worse as the movements spread across the country. That's when the accusation of bigotry became as common as a Keith Olbermann meltdown.

Because of this, I aggressively defended the Tea Partiers on my show. I pointed out how little evidence of bad behavior there was. No doubt there are white people who hate Obama, but it's entirely possible they just hate what he stands for, not his color. Remember, as the movement kicked off, TEA stood for "taxed enough already." That's a coherent, defensible message. What's wrong with starting there, instead of, you know . . . racism claims?

I have a lot of friends who are Tea Partiers, so I took the racist thing seriously. It would "offend" me, to the extent that these critics were smearing people I knew. I didn't like that. One of my closest friends ran two bars in New York. She never engaged in any political activity in her life. She was too busy making a living, providing jobs for blacks, gays, Hispanics, even little people. (On St. Patrick's Day, she hired a leprechaun. The green tights gave me a rash.) So now that she became part of the Tea Party, she's racist? If worrying about the future of our country is racist, then we're all wearing white sheets.

But I also found the charge lazy and dirty. If you call someone racist, you shut down the debate before it ever starts.

A similar thing should happen with the Occupiers. As a protester there, you'd end up spending more time on blogs trying to quell stories of rape, overdoses, and fecal warfare than extolling the movement's attack on corporate greed. That was their racism equivalent. But the criticism was never as bad for the OWSers. The media rarely focused on their scary stuff. A racist sign at a Tea Party meant so much more than murder at an occupation.

Occupy Wall Street is clearly the antithesis to the Tea Partiers. These people are younger, messier, more disorganized, and well, let's face it, cuter, if you like the flea-bitten type. If you brought your "people I would have sex with" geiger counter, you might get more beeps in the beginning of the occupation than at the Tea Party events. Well, unless you're into elegant grannies, which I am. The geiger counter would stop working, however, as the OWS movement went on and on—and the cuties were replaced with transients, junkies, and worse: whiny beta males.

The parallels are obvious. First, there's the age. For every old joke aimed at the Tea Party, you could retort with the naivete of the self-absorbed student. With age comes experience. And with aging, come fanny packs. Young people can happily spend thousands of dollars on electronics and clothes, then complain about economic unfairness. Old people know what it's like when the bill comes. Which is why the young people always seem to have more fun. On the other hand, old folks have forgotten what it's like to be idealistic, to really believe big changes are possible or even advisable. That's wisdom.

The easiest jab against the Occupiers is hygiene. The imagery was vivid: disgusting piles of trash, dirty tents, weird homeless men creeping around for prey. And that was just the press pen. If you didn't see the YouTube video of the dude squatting for a poop in the middle of Occupy Boston, you haven't lived. (Well, maybe you have, but your life is somewhat impoverished.) But I admit that the movement wasn't all about soiling yourself and others—and that it's too easy to dismiss the entire movement over bowel movements. And to their credit, the Occupier phenomenon forced me to read more books about the financial meltdowns. Thanks to all that reading, I now know less than ever, but I sound like I know more.

But we cannot ignore the assaults, rapes, and assorted other criminal acts occurring within these occupations. This was the *real* serious charge against the Occupiers—and the media that coddled them. "Oh, it's just a few bad apples" seemed to be the refrain.

Perhaps the Occupiers initially embraced revolution, but the newer members seemed to embrace a more sordid, violent reality that accompanies said revolution.

This stuff makes the "racist" charge against the Tea Partiers seem tame. For me, I can tolerate one racist among 10,000 old farts, but when a way larger percentage of a movement is made up of anarchists and criminals who want to upend society, there is cause for concern.

This is where the self-examination matters. If the OWS movement admitted to the horrible stuff going on, then I would admire and respect them. But they haven't, so I hate that they adore their ideology so much that they let their own supporters fall victim to assaults by more unsavory members. If I were sitting in a tent with an abuser, I wouldn't just ask him to leave, I'd drag him to the cops by his oily dreads.

The thing that gets me is this simple question: Why does the media prefer one group over the other? Why did the media find the Tea Party hilariously stupid but the Occupiers heroic? If you're liberal, you'll say, "Because the Occupiers are right." But that's not the issue. The issue is excusing mayhem. You can't sit by while bad stuff happens.

Actually, I think I have the answer: The Tea Parties represent your parents; the Occupiers represent sex. One is slow and cranky; the other is brash, young, and unpredictable. The bottom line: One is square, the other is fun. One is clean, the other delightfully dirty.

And so this duopoly presents itself once again. It's not left and right. It's uncool and cool. It's high school. The mainstream media loves the cool, even if we know the uncool end up paying the bills.

For the apologists of the OWS movement, if they had an inspirational figure to look up to, it would have to be Walter Duranty, the creepy writer for the *New York Times* who won awards for whitewashing Soviet crimes. While people died by the millions, he wrote sunnily of the communist utopia, ignoring the multitude of horrors simply because it would destroy the story—the one that says capitalism is evil and socialism is lots better. And if that better way requires hiding the deaths of millions—well, that's not the fault of the system. We'll work out the kinks along the way, so let's not make a big deal out of it, okay? Better to tolerate a little evil if the end result is really good. Besides, I'll win a Pulitzer, and Uncle Josef will like me!

Sound familiar? That's the opinion of every person I talked to about Occupy Wall Street. They all kept accusing me of "cherry-picking" incidents to taint their fluffy, wonderful uprising. To them OWS was the Snuggles Bear, misunderstood. When really it was the Big Bad Wolf, with gastritis.

Mind you, these are the same people who desperately tried to find just one example of a Tea Partier yelling the N-word, and when confronted with the demand to supply one, simply couldn't. On my late-night show back in the fall of 2011, a liberal guest made the startling admission that he had been at a Tea Party and personally witnessed "hours" of racist behavior. I asked him for examples. He demurred. I gently asked again. Nope, he just wasn't going to go there. I texted our ombudsman, who monitors the show for mistakes, and wrote, "Ask this guy again, I don't believe him." So during his segment later in the show, he politely asked this fellow (the author of a wildly successful humor book) for evidence. At this point, the guest looked a little unnerved. And again, the guest pleaded no contest. He wasn't going to offer evidence.

Perhaps because he had none.

Unlike that guest on my show, I find it almost too easy to

chronicle the hundreds of crimes, both big and little, committed by the Occupiers. It's no longer cherry-picking when you've got a truckload of cherries, ready to tip the whole truck over. At Big Hollywood, the late Andrew Breitbart's website, as well as a blog called *Verum Serum,* they catalogued a thousand of them. Here's a sample of cherries:

In Manhattan, cops picked up a twenty-six-year-old Crown Heights man after two women reported two separate sexual assaults. How was he able to commit two, when the first attack was already well known among the camp? Don't ask—you'll just smear the movement.

In Hartford, Connecticut, the cops received a tip about a sexual assault at that camp. The victim was located, and told of a man aggressively groping and kissing her. The victim never called the cops. Why? Well, who wanted to draw negative attention to the movement? Tolerate, tolerate, tolerate.

In Lawrence, Kansas, a sexual assault might have taken place, but Occupiers just aren't sure if the suspect was a member of the group, of course.

Oh yeah, there was a murder in Oakland, at Frank Ogawa Plaza, home to the grittiest of the protests. More crimes followed in Oakland—so many, in fact, it would require another book. Or another Oakland, which is something nobody wants.

Also, in Oakland, activists trashed the outside of a Whole Foods (a tony supermarket catering to customers who embrace social

justice). Men's Wearhouse even closed their store in solidarity with the activists, but that didn't stop protesters from smashing their windows (appeasers always get it in the end, history shows). That could explain why the Occupiers all seemed to be wearing really cheesy suits the next day.

In Spokane, Washington, cops responded to a possible sexual assault. A woman had returned to her tent, only to find some dude running out of it. Inside, a woman was passed out, nude from below the waist.

Back in New York, the *Post* reported a pervert assaulting a woman in her tent one early morning. Protesters chased him out of the park but never bothered to call the cops.

And if you think Sharia law is just a scary thing employed by radical Muslims who eschew the laws of any given country, then you haven't been to the Baltimore protests. There the activists distributed pamphlets telling protesters how to handle sexual assaults among themselves, rather than going to the cops. After this "security statement" was exposed, they revised it to list services victims can use, you know, after they've been victimized. How thoughtful. Repressive tolerance means never having to file a report. OWS was the best thing to happen to perverts since mirrored boots.

That's just a handful. But there are other examples—from your basic vandalism to arson amounting to millions of dollars in damages. Whether it's assaults, rapes, fistfights, pooping, vandalism, or arson, OWS offered a prurient parade of pungent perversion.

Now, you can still favor it over the Tea Party if you want, but since there weren't any rapes, assaults, vandalism, pooping, fist-fights, or arson, you're going to look really stupid (as if that might actually stop Susan Sarandon anyway). Even more, consider how much larger the Tea Party gatherings were and you realize, simply by proportion, that the OWS protesters, pound for pound, had more problems, more perversity, more poop. Maybe the Tea Party events had one bad apple among tens of thousands. Among OWS, the places reeked of rotten cores.

But no one cares—at least in the media. The violence at the protests was the most underreported aspect, even among women reporters. Where were the feminists? Why wasn't anyone worried about the women in these parks? Had they put tolerance before safety?

Or are people just scared? Could it be that if you raise a concern, you're testing your tolerance bona fides? If it means the rich get less rich, the poor get free college tuition, and America becomes the utopia where everyone gets everything they want, minus the notion of hard work—go for it.

But historians know: What begins as a utopian vision, always—*always*—ends in bloodshed. Because you have to force a utopia on a free people. Free people want to pursue their own happiness, but a one-size-fits-all approach requires herding the free, against their will, into the state's idea of what's right. Then it's not utopia. It's Uganda. It's 100 million dead.

And it's not like the folks behind the movement have hidden their intentions. Adbusters, the Canadian activist group, has made it clear: they don't like capitalism, and want revolution. And they know how to foment it. YouTube clip by YouTube clip.

Take the infamous pepper-spraying at UC Davis in November 2011. That was the movement's desirable money shot—it *had* to happen. Sure, it made the cops look bad. That was the goal—to create a David vs. Goliath story. Even though pepper spray was created with the purpose of preventing physical contact that would put people in the hospital, it's considered barbaric.

But there's no permanent damage, the discomfort fades fast, and it effectively de-escalates confrontation. That's what it was invented for. Only the media could elevate pepper spray to a human rights violation. Which denigrates real human rights violations. When you see no distinction between pepper-spraying an unruly protester and Bashar al-Assad killing his fellow Syrians, we're firmly in Walter Duranty territory.

I will wager that most of the students who were sprayed wouldn't have traded that moment for a million bucks. They got instant fame, superiority, sympathy from all the right places. For some majors, they would have earned 16 credits for the arrest. And in twenty years, they will still be bragging about that moment. I'm sure many will brag about being there when they weren't (as seen with 1967's Summer of Love; we would have needed a "half decade of love" to accommodate all who claimed to have been there. Most of them were undoubtedly on their parents' sofa, reading the liner notes for *Meet the Monkees*). As for the actual cause they were protesting, that will be forgotten, for it is far less important than gaining the admiration of their anarchist peers. And later, a job in media or academia.

After all, the actual cause really has no positive goal. It's run by radicals, and radicalism isn't about creating something new, but destroying the old.

Consider: the Americans for Prosperity Conference that happened in D.C., in mid-November 2011. As far as I can tell from reading its press releases, the whole focus of the thing was to promote economic opportunity. These were people who got to-gether to talk about becoming more successful, and helping others become more successful. You know, capitalism.

So what happened? The D.C. protesters descended on the place in an attempt to do . . . what? I'm not sure.

What I did see in the Daily Caller video: hordes of angry left-wing protesters pressing up against the doors of the con-ference building, screaming at and intimidating innocent par-ticipants. This aggressive free-flowing tantrum resulted in two elderly women being injured, one of whom had traveled a dozen hours by bus. I'm sure she was simply a rich bitch capitalist op-pressor. Because, you know, they always take the bus.

And so the protesters' assault revealed their true aims: attack-ing individuals who do, rather than demand. I mean, if you've never made anything in your life—except debt and poorly worded protest signs—I guess it makes sense to go after the doers. OWS became the takers wreaking havoc on the makers.

And so I will cherry-pick once more, because I just can't stop. At a San Diego protest, the activists took up real estate where street cart vendors once had been working. The vendors, in a gesture of goodwill, fed these protesters for free. But when they stopped (inevitably, as handouts must), the protesters became irate. These vendors are no better than the one percent!

The protesters trashed the carts with, among other things, urine and blood. Which, among some Californians, is actually considered street food. This was Greece, in a nutshell. The inci-dent was covered locally, but the mainstream media overlooked this stuff, because, like the protest organizers, they knew it would detract from the positive message. You won't find that example or any of the others I just mentioned in those tony compendiums on the OWS movement. Instead, you'll find inane essays on the importance of the movement written by hipster authors trying to score progressive points. It's the blind writing about the stupid.

Right now we're experiencing the age of anti-bullying enlightenment. This can be a good thing. Bullies suck. But someone needs to explain to me how celebrities can focus on isolated incidents of bullying without condemning this other widespread intimidation. Shouldn't Lady Gaga get out there with a bullhorn?

Better to focus on the peaceful or camera-ready stuff—like when Lou Reed shows up, or Philip Glass decides to do a mic check. Just a month or so prior to me writing this very sentence, David Crosby and Graham Nash performed at a New York protest. I had no idea they were still alive. (Alas, their performance did little to confirm this. Even when captured on videotape.)

THE JOKE STOPS HERE

.

THE FIRST TIME A JOKE WAS EVER TOLD, you can bet someone died from it. They didn't have picket signs or letter-writing campaigns back then, but they had hurt feelings. They registered it by bashing your head in with a club.

My good friend Joe DeRosa is a successful comic and actor who happens to live two floors above me. I see him in the elevator a lot, and we often end up accidentally drunk—before we reach the ground floor. He tells me about a phenomenon called selective listening, when he tells a joke one way but the audience hears it another way.

"I tell a joke about Jesus Christ. Basically I make fun of people who pray to Jesus for stupid shit, when basically this guy died on the cross for their sins. The whole point was, telling people to stop asking this poor guy for shit. He's a tough dude; he had nails hammered into his hands! And you're praying for a job promotion." So what is essentially a salute to Jesus Christ is misconstrued as the opposite, because all people hear is a joke that has Jesus in it. "It doesn't matter what the message of the joke is," Joe says. He says the Jesus joke is his parents' favorite joke, and his dad is a deacon. The fact is, people just get angry, because all they hear is something they believe should make them angry. It's blasphemous, when in reality, it's actually honest and perceptive. Jesus might have laughed.

People get angry not because of the joke but because it hits too close to home. Think about it: When someone cracks a joke, it is meant to be taken as a joke. It's not real. Yet that is ignored—selectively. Offense over a joke is a dog whistle, selectively heard by those with a dog in the hunt. (And if that metaphor confused you, as it did me, you can selectively tune it out.)

Meaning, the same person who laughs uproariously over a joke ridiculing the ethnic background of the scamps on *Jersey Shore* will get pissed when you target the Kardashians. Because they're Armenian, and the offended person had an aunt who was Armenian. Who died in a fire. So you'd better not make any Armenians-who-died-in-a-fire jokes. (There goes half my act.)

Now, should every comedian demand his audience fill out questionnaires regarding areas that are off-limits? Perhaps a checklist that reads, "Are you black, gay, Hispanic, transgender, missing a limb? Do you have a relative with arthritis, have you worked in a labor camp in China, do you have thirty-four toes, can you see colors, do you have a fish-smelling disease or overgrown eyebrows, are you too short for roller coaster rides, do you have an unattractive unibrow or a penis shaped like Florida, do you have a mom who was a prostitute, a sister who was in the Manson family, or a dad who ran Jonestown?"

The assumption is that when someone makes a joke, it's a joke. We're all adults and we understand no one is actually trying to "hurt" someone.

So why the outrage, then? Why does someone get mad when Rush Limbaugh makes a joke about Barack Obama? Why do groups get angry when Louis C.K. unloads a crass, drunken tweet about Sarah Palin? Why did Gilbert Gottfried lose work over earthquake jokes? Why do people have to apologize over things that don't inflict real pain on people?

Perhaps it's not about outrage. In a way, it could be about jealousy, which is the basis of much manufactured grievance. The anger toward a comedian erupts not because the comment simply strikes a nerve, but because the angered person feels unable to say the same thing, and that's unfair. Why should you have the freedom to say something sick, but I can't? I don't mean "won't" or "wouldn't." I mean "can't." It's a joke I can't make, because it might get me in trouble.

See, it's not that people can't say it, it's that people can't take it. So I'll shut up about it.

Sure, I've been guilty of this in the past. Someone will say something I don't like, and I will write something about that person, ridiculing them. Later, I realize I was mad I didn't come up with it first! But I stopped getting outraged, because I realized it wasn't worth it.

First, the worst sin for a comedian is laziness. That explains all the Palin jokes, churned out by the dolts who write Bill Maher's material. But it's nothing to be outraged about, really. And don't get me wrong, I think creepy jokes done on women simply because they're conservative are shitty, but they are far from outrageous. They're just lame. But they are also providing a service. When someone laughs at one of those jokes, you know that person doesn't get out much. In scientific terms, they are called "dumbshits." It's like when dogs sniff each other's asses. This ritual inspection is how they identify each other. Once you hear Maher make a lame Palin joke, you know he's a dope without even having to sniff his ass (the way many of his guests do so painfully on his show). It's a real time-saver!

But if someone writes or tells a joke that's funny, and it's about someone you like, you owe it to yourself to laugh. Sure, you should expect a wider range of targets from today's comics, but don't hold your breath. I'd like Louis C.K. to make fun of Obama as much as he does Palin, but he's a liberal, so he won't. I'd like to see Ricky Gervais make fun of liberals as much as he ridicules the religious, but that's not what he cares about. After a while fans of Gervais like me will find his schtick tiresome, but he doesn't care, nor should he. He is obsessed with atheism, and what he perceives as the harmful effects of religion—and so what? The existence of God and the origins of the universe are the real questions that keep us up at night, so why shouldn't he devote all his talents to that? It's not offensive as long as he makes me laugh and think, or even get angry. But yeah, it can get tiresome. And he may end up being pretentious, like if you saw his cover shot on *The Humanist* magazine, in which he was crucified—the nadir of his self-satisfied martyr complex. I'd still love him though. Were I capable of love.

The second worst reaction is to turn into a prude bent on admonishment. When you watch Bill Maher's *Real Time* and he goes there yet again, calling Palin a twat, or Bachmann a bitch, turn off your outrage meter. Instead feel satisfied in the fact that Maher has lost whatever gift he had for real ridicule. And watch something else, for God's sake, like *Hoarders*. Now there's feel-good television. It makes me feel well adjusted. And it's cheaper than paying a therapist.

ROLL MODELS

IT WAS A STORY DESIGNED TO OUTRAGE right-wing nut-bags like me. According to *LA Weekly,* a former "porn star" appeared at an elementary school in Compton, California, to read to children.

The porn star is not just any old worn-out slapper—it's Sasha Grey, a "new kind" of adult actress, who prides herself in doing both hard-core stuff and mainstream muck. She's a jackoff-of-all-trades, if you will. Because of her unique persona, she became the obsession of Steven Soderbergh, who devoted a whole movie to her (I confess to not seeing it—I'm waiting for the musical). He must have found her fascinating, as men with film cameras often do when they come across a hot chick who will screw men with film cameras.

Later, still enthralling Hollywood types, she showed up on that outdated tripe called *Entourage,* playing herself (why not?—she's so cool!), and the object of the star's affections. Her ability to use her sexual confidence to control men was seen as heroic.

The fact is, Grey is famous not because she does porn, she's famous because she's cute, and makes it acceptable to do porn. Trafficking in nonporn arenas makes her other stuff seem cool. It's like, "I'm not just an actress, I also do anal, and vice versa."

Actually, she's likely famous because she screws powerful Hollywood men, but whatever. More important, she's still young and hot—not worn-out, drug-addicted, and suicidal like most porno queens. Give her five years and she'll be more weathered than Ed Schultz.

Yes, this isn't gramps's porn star. Which is why the whole controversy over her reading to kids in Compton seems totally calculated. It's all part of the "Sasha Grey as performance art" piece that has now become her "edgy" life. And all of this is predicated, remember, on the idea that she can actually read. Most of her films don't involve a lot of complex dialogue.

Now, I suppose this is all about second chances, and just because Sasha Grey did porn (extensively), why shouldn't she read to kids? I'll tell you why. As far I as can tell, Grey has never disowned her porn history—and believe me, I did the research to back up that fact. Weeks of it, in fact. I'm still doing it now.

She parlayed her porno past and present into getting work outside porn. It's a neat little trick. Do the obscene first, in order to go mainstream—knowing that obscenity is the novelty. Who knew going hardcore meant you could work with the guy who directs *Oceans Eleven*? And that's how she ended up on *Entourage,* a show so dumb it's closed-captioned for rocks.

So to me, Sasha's is a really positive message to today's young lasses: You can do porn and maybe live past thirty. Which as you know (or I know), is the God's honest truth! Unless you've got a laptop, and can Google "dead porn stars," where in an instant you'll find a ream of websites listing the lurid manner in which these sex workers end up. Ironically, there are no happy endings. Usually, it's suicide, overdoses, and accidents. I couldn't find many "natural causes" in the mix, mainly because you have to live long enough to qualify. I've said it before, in the adult film industry, forty is the new dead.

But that doesn't matter. Because in the world of tolerance, pointing out this sober fact makes you seem narrow-minded and hurtful. You are intolerant if you don't let a girl who just had a thirty-six-member gang bang read "Jack and Jill" to your little runt.

And so this stupid porn star story was precisely manufactured crud designed to make you feel stodgy and mean if you think some lifestyles should prevent you from commingling with impressionable youth.

See, as an "enlightened" individual, you're supposed to nod along with these exercises in repressive tolerance. And really, that's all the exercise is designed for—for others who abide by this PC nonsense, while also tweaking your moral sensibilities and calling you out for your outdated intolerance. It's an exercise in superiority by witless cranks who would rather deny real truth about life. Better to appear cool and wrong than right and intolerant. Sasha Grey can do all the porn she wants. Just don't involve kids in your PR stunts.

Never mind that if you asked a porn star if she'd want her own child to be in porn, she'd say hell no. If she lives to have kids, that is. In fact, I doubt this statement has ever been uttered in the history of humankind: "This is my mom; she's a porn star. I'm so glad she came to my graduation today." And Mom, please don't gang-bang the faculty.

So what message does this send to girls at that school? Now, for boys the usual "role model" you'd find in a classroom on career day might be a fireman, a cop, or a well-known late-night commentator who can squat twice his own weight. But all the "outside talent coordinator" could get to represent inspiring women . . . is a porn star? And yes, the school district apparently had an "outside talent coordinator." Only in California could such an alternate universe exist. Who the hell is paying for that? (If you live in California, take a wild guess.) Bottom line: Forget fields like medicine or law. You should really be looking to the porn dens of the San Fernando Valley for your career inspiration.

And you wonder why kids are screwed these days—that's what their role models do for a living.

The tale of Sasha Grey speaks to a larger debate about porn. What used to be a shameful career, and a hobby kept hidden, is now part of our everyday life. Porn stars show up on reality and talk shows. They make cameo appearances in movies and show up at comedy roasts. If you voice any concern about this, you're the crank. And I am a crank. On my show, I make no bones about my dislike for porn, only because I've seen enough of it to choke a chicken. (Yeah, I'm a hypocrite, but admitting it is the first step to enlightenment.) But we live in a time when the person extolling personal virtue is seen as an idiot, and the star of a gang bang an inspirational trailblazer. This is not progress. It's just another step in the direction of a shame-free society, where every behavior is excused because we're just too cowardly to do anything else but pass the lube. Which is a long way of saying: California.

THE PIG PASS

IT WAS A FIRST OF ITS KIND: an "ambush by house band." Back in November 2011, congresswoman Michele Bachmann, then a presidential candidate, appeared on the Jimmy Fallon show. Someone must have told her that this adventure would help her faltering presidential run. That someone was probably high.

When she walked out onto the set, the house band, called The Roots, accompanied her entrance with a song whose title rhymes with "Lyin' Ass Bitch." Because it was "Lyin' Ass Bitch."

This little prank created an uproar on the right, and also on the left (for once), prompting some feminists (usually quiet about this crap happening to conservative women) to say that the band's choice of music was wrong—even if you find Bachmann's stances on various issues objectionable.

Fallon did apologize later, after the brouhaha. He did so profusely, even if it was on Twitter—that new wussy path of phony penance. (How did people apologize before social networks? Send smoke signals?)

Questlove, the Roots joint front man and drummer, defended himself, saying it was all in good fun. He wanted everyone to see how clever he was—tickled pink about his little plan to put one over on the hapless congresswoman. Which makes him a coward. It also makes him a political idiot. Even if you don't like Bachmann's positions, no one's accused her of being a liar before.

I can't say I'm outraged over this prank—because then I'm a hypocrite. After all, my thesis is that most outrage is manufactured for emotional release and attention gratification, so I can't start screaming about this. And I'll admit, choosing covert songs is clever. (What goes with Ambassador Bolton? "I Am the Walrus"?) But if you're going to attack someone, do it to their face, not with a song.

I work in TV. And I know the green room where the guests wait is always close to the studio. Questlove could have easily stopped by and said, "Hey, Congresswoman Bachmann, I want to tell you that I find your political stance on gay marriage disgusting, and I'm going to register my disgust on the show in a manner that will not affect your interview. I'm just doing this so my friends will think I'm clever!"

If he had said that, then he wouldn't be a coward. But he didn't do that, so he's a coward. Even more, the choice of song was a bad one, for another reason: When someone disagrees with your beliefs but can't explain why, their fallback position is always, "He lies." That somehow exempts them from formulating a counterargument or anything remotely close to an intellectual response. Questlove calling Bachmann a "lyin' ass bitch" makes him both crude and stupid. I bet if you asked Questlove what Bachmann "lies" about, he wouldn't have an answer. Which is why he was probably too scared to approach her in the green room. And this makes him the little "bitch" of the story.

What's truly amazing is how the left seems baffled by the revulsion it causes. Think about Bill Maher's disbelief whenever something he says about women is seen as misogynistic. Or that weird "slut" attack on Laura Ingraham by Ed Schultz.

To them it's daring comedy. Why is that? It's because liberals are surrounded by liberals all day, and so they develop a massive blind spot concerning what's acceptable to everyone else. I call it Bad Taste Blind Spot Disorder, or BTBSD. (It's not just an acronym, it's also the sound I make when I'm eating borscht.)

When you suffer from BTBSD, you essentially spend all your time around people who share your assumptions, which makes it exceedingly easy for you to say what's on your mind. You sit around all day and tell rape jokes about conservatives. And then, whoops—one day you make the mistake of telling that joke outside your bubble, unaware of its effect. And it pisses people off. The joke falls flat, and you're miffed. And if you have a smidgen of self-awareness, you're embarrassed, too.

This is Bill Maher's life.

That's why, on *The View,* when Elisabeth Hasselbeck confronted Maher about a rape joke he told about her, he felt like he was the victim. "It was just a joke," his pained face kept reminding us, deeply disappointed that his segment was now being wasted having to answer for his lax attitudes about rape jokes— and defending how funny his rape humor is.

True, Maher didn't really want Hasselbeck raped. But that's not the point. The point is, Maher's persona and his brownnosing audience make him susceptible to saying crap—crap that he wouldn't say about Michelle Obama, Nancy Pelosi, or any other liberal woman. It's only right-wing females he targets.

But worse than Maher, on *The View,* were Hasselbeck's cohosts. While she took the comic to task for his joke, none of her female pals chimed in to agree. They, like Maher, simply squirmed.

And Hasselbeck was doing what they would never do at one of their all-lib cocktail parties: calling someone out for being an ass.

When it comes down to it, the real babies, the real whiners, the real "bitches" are lefty celebrities. And the media and the feminist movement give them all a pass. The result? Frothy, infantile, embarrassing man-babies, like the charming comedic actor Alec Baldwin.

I mean, if I ask you what kind of a celebrity male—in his mid-fifties—would throw a tantrum on a plane because he couldn't play his computer game, the answer will always be Alec Baldwin. Now, if you remember, Baldwin was one of those mega-celebs who aligned themselves with the Occupy protesters, effectively giving his own repulsive behavior a pass by the tolerati.

So this guy—a self-proclaimed champion of the working class—feels totally entitled to ridicule the working class (i.e., a flight attendant), slamming a plane restroom door so loud it alerts the pilot. (That's just what we need in the post-9/11 world—adult celebrities throwing tantrums in planes.) If this were anyone else who did not possess Alec's liberal bona fides, he would have been roundly humiliated by the late-night comics. Instead, however, he gets a spot on *Saturday Night Live* to poke fun at his own tantrums. He took his boorish behavior and made it instantly adorable! Because, being a lefty, he could.

But if you think about it, maybe Baldwin is the real hero in all this. Someone has to stand up for self-absorbed petulant stars who can't go a single minute without instant mindless gratification. Sure, his behavior delayed the departure for all other passengers, but he's allowed that luxury. Because he is both a feminist and a greenie (despite flying coast to coast frequently), the rules of hypocrisy are suspended. Crusading as a phony bleeding heart allows you to be a real-life asshole. And so Baldwin can ridicule the working class and use up all the airline fuel he wants—because, above all else, *he cares.* Repressive tolerance gives him a pass. Yep, if you care about the things Alec cares about, then all of his behavior is tolerated, permitted, and inevitably encouraged. Like he wasn't an asshole enough—we gotta encourage him now? You just know no one has told Alec no. And if they did, he'd just find someone else who'd say yes. There are pages and pages in the back of the *Village Voice* that cater to it. (But those people never look as good in real life as they do in their ad. Trust me.)

HARMED FORCES

I LOVE A MAN IN UNIFORM. And I'm not talking about my house-boys (sarongs hardly qualify as a uniform). But for the left, toler-ance is rarely afforded to the military. Because, you know, they kill people. And they kill people better than anyone. To the left, that's bad. In their world, an American military would not exist. Instead, we'd send "peace armies" to foreign nations to teach them how to weave hemp skirts and condemn patriarchy.

But the rest of us know that there's no point having a military if they aren't doing what they're supposed to do. It's like buying a Maserati and keeping it in the garage. Getting rid of the bad guys is their vocation—which they do, awesomely. If there are any competent Americans left in America—or the world, for that matter—it's our military. God bless them. If only the rest of gov-ernment worked half as well. But the fact is, the bad guys our military are fighting seem to be getting more love these days, es-pecially on college campuses. And the better they are at their job, the more crap the military gets.

Back in January 2012, a video surfaced featuring a group of American soldiers pissing on some Taliban corpses. When I first saw the video, it made me uneasy.

Which totally makes sense. As a human being, when you see

something out of the ordinary—a thing that doesn't occur in your normal life—it's bound to shock and confuse you. So I get the revulsion. The video features two things few people find pleasure in looking at: men urinating publicly and dead bodies. Both gross, to say the least. Both things cause psychological discomfort when seen. Put them together, they cause an immediate, visceral reaction.

One loud "yuck."

While this is an understandable and perfectly natural reaction, please remember, War is yuck.

And, no doubt, what they did was wrong. I get it, it's disgusting to pee on corpses, but I don't get the outrage from the media and the left concerning *how* disgusting it is. And while I don't get the outrage, I'm used to it: whenever anything negative pops up surrounding the military, the left never lets it go to waste. They hate our awesome military, for it represents how awesome America is, which they hate, too. In a perfect world, America would be powerless, without a military, and our enemies would crush us. Because in a progressive world, we deserve every bit of it.

The media revulsion regarding the video, though, reminds me of bystanders who yell at a police officer as he tries to cuff a PCP-addled perp. They react to the violence of the event without understanding what the job requires to maintain order or keep you safe. Do not expect Miss Manners to kill bad guys or wage war.

My primitive concept of war is that it's at its most merciful when it's over fast—which requires an impulse to shred your enemy to pieces, then howl like a crazy person at the moon.

You send a twenty-year-old to war, who is trained to think this way, do not expect civility.

And instead of condemning them, maybe consider what you would do in similar circumstances . . . if you could even stand it.

Of course I don't condone the behavior, but I *understand* it. Even if you've never been to war (like me), you know that a war-like mentality allows for a whole host of unusual behaviors. If you saw these behaviors on a street in your hometown, they would seem odd. Pissing on a corpse in Green Bay—is weird. Pissing on a corpse in Afghanistan after a firefight—it's unseemly, but I'm not there for the whole movie. Pissing on a person pretending to be a corpse below Manhattan's Twenty-third Street—45 dollars.

But you won't find that sensible understanding from the left. Which I'd accept—if they were consistent about all types of atrocity.

Here's where the tolerant left falls apart once again. You never see them express outrage when our enemies behead, mutilate, or hang our soldiers. You never hear them express outrage over what these beasts do to women, gays, and whomever else they consider worthless, according to their caveman mentality. They are vicious, backward, murderous assholes—but according to the left, our guys are worse because they peed on those assholes' corpses. (By the way, here's another bizarre inconsistency: How is pissing on a corpse worse than turning that guy into a corpse? I mean, we accept that our troops go there to kill people, and I can safely say that being killed has to be worse than getting splashed with urine. It defies logic that drones are preferable to water sports!)

I think the wisest commentary came from war hero and all-around badass Representative Allen West, who wrote in a letter to *The Weekly Standard:*

> The Marines were wrong. Give them a maximum punishment under field grade level Article 15 (non-judicial punishment), place a General Officer level letter of reprimand in their personnel file, and have them in full dress uniform stand before their

Battalion, each personally apologize to God, Country, and Corps videotaped and conclude by singing the full US Marine Corps Hymn without a teleprompter.

As for everyone else, unless you have been shot at by the Taliban, shut your mouth, war is hell.

My God. I love this guy. When the hell is he going to run for president? The whole Middle East would be calling us "sir." You think Allen West goes on an apology tour if he makes president? Only to accept some.

So I'll take his opinion over the hand-wringing by the disgusted folks who only take an interest when whatever's discussed reflects badly on the military.

This is because the military kills people, which is intolerant, and involves the following value judgment: "They should die so we can live." Thanks to tolerance, Venezuela's president isn't fertilizer, Ahmadinejad isn't the beloved martyr of Shia wife-beaters everywhere, and every Iraq war movie has the following subtext: "Our culture is no better than theirs—we just have bigger guns." And yes, we got bin Laden, but that was thanks to methods that were once considered by the now victorious administration as outrageous and, well, intolerant. If they'd listened to their own advice, bin Laden would still be breathing, and watching MSNBC.

And for some, the military's main objective—to efficiently kill while preserving their own safety—is made secondary to tolerance. It's all about equality, not victory. Who cares if we're no longer awesomely deadly? We're awesomely correct! Why, we're so awesomely correct, we'll let Major Hasan correspond with Anwar al-Awlaki!

As I write this, Congress still officially bans women from serving in combat roles. But this may be changing, with California Democratic congresswoman Loretta Sanchez having prepared an amendment to the defense budget bill that would change all that. Now, before I tell you why this is a lousy, stupid idea, I want to say that I adore women in the military (particularly the ones with pixie haircuts who can kick my ass—it's a thing I've been into since I saw *Tank Girl* as a boy) and salute their amazing service for our country. But I'm not going to let politically correct notions of "what's fair" undermine my basic common sense about biology, about the sexes, and about how important women are above and beyond combat. They aren't here to kill, they're here to create. But men? Men are earth's Doritos.

That's the simple biological fact. With one male you can create a city—a heterosexual boob creates enough sperm to populate Manhattan (and some men have tried—a shout-out to Eliot Spitzer). But women only have two eggs percolating at a time (I love when I attempt to write coherently about science), and so you need plenty of women to keep the species going. The role of women dictates the role of men: we fight so they don't have to. In essence, they're just more valuable.

There's this metaphor I always bring up, which I stole from a mathematician. Imagine a man and a women enter a casino with a thousand dollars. The woman has two five-hundred-dollar coins; the guy has a thousand one-dollar coins. That casino is life, with all its reproductive options. This is why women are more scrupulous about the choices they make (they incur more loss with less choice), and why they're so damn important. Men, with a thousand one-dollar coins, can pretty much gamble all over the place, even with their lives. That's why so many of them die building bridges, mining for coal, replicating *Jackass* stunts (which men do for the attention of women), and yeah—war. Women shouldn't be in the fighting part of that business, but the tolerati declare that we must overlook this whole biology business.

And here I thought it was the right who denied science. I mean, come on, liberals: if science tells you women are more valuable, denying that is worse than refuting evolution, global warming, the moon landing, and unicorn villages living under the Atlantic combined. (Note: The unicorn villages are indeed real. Try the seahorse sushi.)

Yeah, that sounds unfair and intolerant, and I'm a complete Neanderthal. But the only way we got from being Neanderthals to now—is that women didn't fight.

Let me use an analogy—clumsy as it is—that I've used a dozen times on TV and at bars when I'm too drunk to shut up.

Imagine if your favorite football team decided to allow women to play, to champion equality. Now imagine they do that despite *no other* team following suit. So the Steelers have women in the backfield, and what happens? They get destroyed by the Raiders, who kept an all-male team. You lose. That doesn't matter, though, in the war against intolerance and inequality. Now imagine that the Steelers are the U.S. Marines, and the Raiders are the Iranian Revolutionary Guard. You think those Iranians are going to "sub" in women because the Marines did? Yeah, I've noticed how tolerant they've been in the past. They only kill women when they're victims of rape—a tribute to total tolerance, for it includes a tolerance of rape. The only way Iranian women see combat is as human shields. Otherwise, they're in the rear with the gear, as the saying goes. In fact, in Iran they are the gear.

So we can put women on the front lines but our enemies don't have to. And I don't care how tough a 200-pound woman is—a 200-pound man will win. (I've tested this out in a number of contexts and can more or less confirm its accuracy.) But we've come to realize that, these days, winning isn't on the chalkboard. Repressive tolerance is.

The saddest thing is, the one agent that preserves our ability to be tolerant wusses is our hugely intolerant military. Our military is intolerant of bad guys, and kills them. And somehow that's horrible. And where does it culminate?

Let's turn to the professors at the University of Washington's Department of Global Health, who, according to a story on mynorthwest.com, believe that military recruiters are no different from sexual predators in their "grooming" behavior of students. A young guy serving our country is just like a member of the North American Man/Boy Love Association. Probably worse. Certainly in the eyes of this "tolerant" professor, who probably sees NAMBLA as falsely maligned (and perhaps understaffed).

To back up this innovative claim, the researchers point out that recruiters are encouraged to get involved during field trips and do the scorekeeping—which is what pedophiles might do in order to entice new victims.

But let me point out, it's what parents do, too. And uncles like me (I'm not allowed anywhere near AYSO soccer matches since the incident with the oranges). But the professors left that piece out, for it would have ruined their atrocious exercise in moral relativism.

So what does this tell you? Well, that academics can say just about anything they want about the military, because by virtue of their vocation, they are not required to allot the same benevolent tolerance you would give to other groups—like gang members, inmates, Occupy protesters, or San Francisco nudists. Because, after all, American soldiers probably kill innocent women and babies. They don't deserve the tolerance you'd give to, say, a terrorist those troops are trying to capture. That's the true, insidious irony: the left is more tolerant of the people who want us dead than they are of the people trying to protect us from those who want us dead. This intolerant view toward our most giving citizens is never exemplified by your average American, but is expressed only in secluded teachers' lounges populated by men in their forties who still think a ponytail makes a statement about colonialism.

On that note, let's head over to Iowa State University during the wintry months of 2011. That's when Townhall.com reported that the College Republicans kicked off their annual Support Our Troops Care Package Drive to gather donations for stuff to send to troops overseas for the holidays. It's the usual stuff: trail mix, candy, socks, stocking caps, foot powder, toothpaste, puzzle books, and wet wipes. (I hear wet wipes are treated like gold overseas, which is understandable—they've made my life a lot easier when I forget to do laundry.) Now, normal people would find this drive to collect stuff for the troops to be wholly positive. But academics are not normal people. They are not even people in my book (see my book, *Academics: Rodents Masquerading as Humans*). Here is "instructor" Thomas Walker, who wrote a letter to the school paper mocking the endeavor. In it, he said, "Aren't GIs paid enough to buy what they need, and even what they want? . . . What are the troops doing for us? Nothing. But against us they're doing a lot: creating anti-American terrorists in the countries they occupy."

Oh yes, there's that *occupy* verb again. Why is it when you hear that word, it's always coming from a tenured, self-absorbed twit whose achievements are measured by years of not working? And dandruff?

My gut tells me this creep only wrote this letter to impress naive coeds who fall for anything that might be considered deep.

And unfortunately, to a lot of America's current student body, this nonsense qualifies. And a lot of repressive tolerance rhetoric is geared toward that—your condemnation of injustice, masked as traditional American values, makes you a winner at cocktail parties, coffee shops, and Green Day mosh pits. The instructor wrote this pap because he felt he could write this pap. He must have felt really special when he pressed send.

Repressive tolerance, among the dumb and gullible, gets you laid. Isn't that why most of these guys become academics? The girls stay the same age—as the academics get older and smellier. You fashion some fashionable hate, and that coed (it's her first time away from home) can find you really "deep."

This condemnation of charity toward our military repeated itself, according to FoxNews.com, at a place called Suffolk University, in Boston, where another professor became enraged over student groups sending care packages to troops over Christmas. So he sent an e-mail to his colleagues saying how awful it would be to help those who have gone "overseas to kill other human beings." The college didn't reprimand the professor, which led to a resignation from another member of the faculty, who was irrationally upset, of course. That guy must be the truly intolerant one. Don't these assholes have classes to teach and papers to grade? That's the problem with professors and actors. Too much time to demonstrate to us what jackasses are.

Academia traffics in the illusion of tolerance. But the stereotype of the college campus as a place where ideas can flourish is bullpoop. Sure, if you believe Che Guevara is awesome and al Qaeda just a subversive reaction to American hegemony, that's cool. But if you're young and conservative, the tolerant become intolerant. Conservative groups get kicked off campus, the ROTC gets banned from schools, and speakers are harassed or hit with pies. The world of the open-minded suddenly shuts closed when faced with people who don't match their assumptions about how much America sucks. Our campuses have gone from incubators of first-class talent to Useful-Idiot-U. And the Occupy Wall Streeters are shocked they can't get jobs? They'll be lucky to be churning out iPads in a Shanghai sweatshop in a few years.

For another sordid example of repressive tolerance, witness an event at Columbia University, where Anthony Maschek, a student and veteran of the Iraq War, got a not-so-warm greeting. He was recently awarded something inconsequential—I believe it's called a Purple Heart—after being shot eleven times in Iraq. Sure, he's no 50 Cent, but he spent two years at Walter Reed National Military Medical Center and still gets around in a wheelchair. Maschek was speaking at the school, on the topic of getting the ROTC program back on campus.

While trying to explain the need for a strong military, he was shouted at and openly mocked. It was a greeting you'd expect from people who've never done anything remotely sacrificial for their country. The media reaction to this was, of course, decidedly sparse. Obama must've told a joke about bowling that day or something.

Fact is, we live in a culture where reality TV trumps reality, patriotism seems quaint, and no-talent teenyboppers gain more respect and adulation than our boys at war. And remember, this was Columbia, where Mahmoud Ahmadinejad was encouraged to speak (tolerance!), and a guy risking his life to protect your right to speak—is heckled. After all, you can't tolerate someone you've spent you're whole life stereotyping. If you listened to him, your world would fall apart faster than a European economy. In fact, just the sight of anything that smacks of defending your country is seen as "shameful." While you must tolerate all sorts of bizarre beliefs on campus, the idea of allowing our young men and women to simply show up in uniform is abominable.

And this crap is happening even before college. Let's go to Schuylkill Valley High School (something I often say to myself) in Leesport, Pennsylvania, where, according to the *Reading Eagle,* two students were banned from walking across the stage during their graduation because they had donned military sashes, given to them by evil army recruiters as a way to honor their up-and-coming military service. You think these kids would've gotten the same reaction if they were wearing antiwar buttons?

So what's wrong with the folks who banned the sashes? Nothing—they just suck. Brainwashed by the last thirty years of PC dogma, they're suffering from the backward paralysis of tolerance: I'm sure if the two students had decided to arrive cross-dressed as their favorite Golden Girl, it would have been perfectly fine. I would have been fine with both, actually. I am a fan of both the military and the Golden Girls. Both were tough bastards.

But apparently the superintendent of the high school claimed they didn't want to honor one group and disappoint another. What a big, giant pussy.

Now, I could ask why so many academics suck. The answer would be, they're jerks, pure and simple. But instead, I imagine these people just don't know anyone who served in the military, and therefore believe the military cannot be a good thing. Remember, deconstructing *Moby-Dick* as a homoerotic thesis is far more important than eradicating the number-one threat to our way of life. Cocooned in their own world, surrounded by people who agree with them, they cannot imagine anyone finding their opinions unoriginal—or, better, repulsive. They deserve a one-way ticket to some hellhole where only the military they detest so strongly can extract them (I'm thinking Walmart on Black Friday). They should be forced to squat in a desert gully and explain to armed enemy combatants whose minds are in the seventh century why their understanding of "the whiteness of the whale" means he shouldn't be executed.

But the lesson learned for all of us is simple and obvious: Tolerance can only be applied to certain groups deemed appropriate by the left. You can tolerate criminals. You can sympathize with brutal thugs on death row. You can even argue that society is guilty for encouraging the crimes of even our worst offenders. But if you choose to serve your country, you lose all rights to be tolerated and do not even deserve a free wet wipe. And that, my friend, is the sound of a civilization turning on itself.

THE SONG REMAINS SO LAME

THE BIGGEST LIE IN POP CULTURE? Rock stars are rebels. *Please,* they're about as edgy as Hostess Snowballs. Case in point: Whenever there's an election, and Republicans are looking for music for their campaign events, you see the same stupid story rear its stupid head. A candidate will use a song in an ad, by aging everyman Bruce Springsteen, or Tom Petty (who is beginning to look like your aunt Sally, assuming your aunt Sally is a cabbage), and what follows is a "how dare they!" uproar—not just from the artists themselves but from the media, too. In sum, they are saying, "Hold on a second, you dorky right-winger! You do not have a free pass with pop culture! Sure, you enjoy much of the same stuff we do, but unlike us, you aren't cool. And when you aren't cool—well, then, we don't have to tolerate you. Yep, we will tolerate almost anything, but not you listening to Fleetwood Mac." (Which actually hasn't been cool since the Carter administration.)

The entertainment industry hates the uncool (read: the right) so much that if a maniacal leader arose from the left to announce he would send the uncool to "how to be cool" camps, no one in a band would raise an objection. They're all about peace and love, as long as it's their peace and love. But if you voted for Bush, you should probably die. Horribly, perhaps by listening to Fleetwood

Mac. I'd say about six minutes of any Stevie Nicks solo album should do it.

Back in 2008, running against Barack Obama, the coolest of the cool, Senator John McCain's campaign decided to use the song "Running on Empty," by doe-eyed simpleton Jackson Browne. McCain ended up having to settle out of court with Browne for not asking permission first (thus providing Browne with his first revenue since 1982). Both the Foo Fighters (that band with the guy from that other band where the dude blew his brains out) and John Cougar Mellencamp (three names linked together to spell "crap") also told McCain to stop using their stuff. And in the 2012 campaign Tom Petty sent a "cease and desist" letter to Michele Bachmann, telling her to stop playing "American Girl." Now this could all be just a legal maneuver—an attempt to block people from using your music without paying—but funny that Obama didn't have that problem. He could have chosen any song from the last fifty years and you know the band would have given interviews talking about how "proud and honored" they were. If you remember (and I do), Springsteen was outraged Reagan used "Born in the U.S.A." in his campaign. (I wonder if Springsteen feels differently now that everyone in what was once called the Soviet Union can buy his songs with a click of a finger.) And as I edit this book, Dee Snider, front man and aged crone from Twisted Sister, just demanded that the Republican VP candidate Paul Ryan stop using their one and only decent song, "We're Not Gonna Take It" on his campaign stops. To be sure, a gratified America quietly applauded the news.

Does this happen on the other side? Do pop stars get upset when a lefty uses their song to get votes? I haven't heard of a single case, but Obama used "The Rising" without Springsteen caring, Bill Clinton played Fleetwood Mac's "Don't Stop" until our ears bled through our noses, and John Edwards played "Our Country" by John Cougar Mellancamp during his ill-fated campaign, without a peep. These musicians were apparently outraged by the right's desire to use their music, but okay with Edwards? John Edwards, adulterer, liar, and weirdo. I've seen holograms more real than this ambulance-chasing lowlife. That this sociopath gets an easier time from the music industry than a war hero like John McCain tells you everything you need to know about dumbass rock stars.

So what do all these bands have in common? They love to see themselves as truly tolerant, but if they ever ran into someone who voted conservative and happened to like their music, they'd probably hit them in the face with their freshly purchased copy of *Dreams from My Father*. So why does musicians' tolerance only flow one way? Well, perhaps they know that if one of their songs shows up in Republican ads, they will get an army of cold shoulders at a Brentwood cocktail party, or worse, one less blow job from a groupie. And in a way, I don't blame them. If I were an artist, I wouldn't want my music associated with any political figure—unless, of course, we exhumed Ronald Reagan and ran him again. But they should operate this method of intolerance for both parties: no one can use my music, period.

That doesn't happen. And this means something more than just what's played in stupid commercials or rallies. Fact is, the real war over hearts and minds these days is not in politics but in pop culture. As Andrew Breitbart once said, politics is downstream from pop culture, not the other way way around.

You can tell your kids day and night to be good people—don't do drugs and or have sex with their ninth-grade teachers—but you're up against some serious competition: Lady Gaga, hip-hop, and anything that passes for entertainment on MTV. Bottom line: What is considered cool is everything you find detrimental to sound living. And boring.

The problem here is that lefties don't grow out of this phase. For most of us, our vision of what is "cool" is established when we're adolescents. But by the time you're in your mid-twenties or so, you should start to realize that what was cool at seventeen should be decidely less so. Certainly by thirty you should be out of your parents' basement. But the hard left somehow manages to see what the rest of us call "growing up" as "selling out." "Hey, if Mellancamp Cougar John can have his adolescence extended indefinitely, why can't I?" Because you're not a millionaire rock star, ya jackass. You're a mailroom clerk with two kids who probably shouldn't have so many Coldplay posters up in his bedroom.

And as for the musicians themselves, let's face facts: what substitutes for hits and genuine cultural relevance for fading rock stars is strident political statements. Outrage at the right's use of a former rock star's music is really "Let me make as much noise about this as I can, because I'm one step from an oldies revue on the outskirts of Branson." Or put more simply, "Hey, remember me? I matter!" It's selling out, but in a way that's acceptable to the left.

But the real truth: Being conservative is a rebellion against predictable rebellion. It's more daring to be traditional than to subvert tradition.

Musicians don't want righties using their music, but would they demand you take off the shirt that has their name on it? Unless you had great breasts, no, because that money goes right into their designer pockets. Point is, they make a stand, when they're not being paid. Bruce will still take your money when you buy that overpriced ticket to Madison Square Garden, whether you voted for Obama or not.

As a host of a late-night show, I've seen the convulsions that occur when I have someone "cool" on. After I had a reviewer of alternative music on my show, a legendary alt-rock producer ripped him for coming on. In effect, this was no different from the high school head cheerleader telling you not to hang out with the chess club.

When I had the Florida metal band known as Torche on the same show, similar crap occurred. Torche is an amazing doom metal/pop hybrid, making some of the best music in the world, if you had that kind of childhood. Their lead singer, Steve Brooks, is like a gay version of Jack Black, only more talented and charming. And hairier. I wanted to capture how cool they were as a band, so I created a video about the band. It went crazy on the Web, as all truly subversive things should. But some people in pop circles were disgusted by what they could not understand. This just didn't fit into their comfy worldview. How could you link a metal band that has a gay singer to a crazy rightie like me? My answer is, You pukes—why not? I'm a right-wing nut and I'm far more tolerant, it turns out, than edgy music bloggers who shoot pool, listen to bootlegs of early Can, and make no money while their girlfriends grow exceedingly exhausted by their promises of self-sufficiency someday. My God, if we knew the Internet would lead to such a raft of self-indulgent pointlessness, we might have asked Al Gore to come up with something else.

There was nothing funnier than watching the liberal convulsion on the music blogs when it was discovered that Moe Tucker, of the legendary band The Velvet Underground, turned out to be a modern-day Tea Partier. If you don't know her, she was the drummer for the hippest band of all time, managed by Andy Warhol, with members including Lou Reed, Nico, and John Cale. It was an inspiration to disaffected slackers, no band was cooler, and just about every group you hear these days ripped them off. Me, I am a huge fan of anything that sounds like them, even if I find Lou Reed about as charming as a cat in a blender. Which is an apt description of his collaboration with Metallica.

But in 2010, bloggers found out that Moe had hit a Tea Party rally, where, like everyone else there, she railed against the direction of this country. The problem was, she didn't fall into the typical definition of the liberal-approved Tea Party stereotype. Moe is way more subversive than the critics of the Tea Party ever could be. So what happens when the coolest cucumber rejects those precious values held by the vintage-T-shirt-wearing, status quo left? Let repressive tolerance commence. Here are a few laments from web-based whiners after discovering Moe ain't like her (or him), and worse—that she had possibly worked at Walmart:

> I was really really heartbroken cause I love her solo albums and had always interpreted the lyrics to be fairly liberal. I am spending the day in mourning for Moe.

> I wouldn't put it past Wal-Mart to put an additive in the employee's water fountains that turns them into tea-partiers.

(One wonders what additives this writer has been adding to her water.)

Of course, once hipsters arbitrarily decide that Walmart is cool to shop at, things will change. Remember how low-class Pabst Blue Ribbon was? Now it's in every hand of every dweeb trying to grow a beard in Brooklyn.

Here's another:

> Lots of working stiffs are Tea Party members, more fools they, so
> if indeed it's Tucker she's just getting shafted by a new boss now.

("More fools they"? Okay there, Falstaff.)

Yep, she made music you loved, but now that she doesn't share your assumptions about politics, she must be stupid, a fool, brainwashed by "the man." I'm telling you, we should've told Gore, "No thanks." Here's a more sympathetic comment:

> I still love Moe . . . I can only hope that she, like so many others,
> are being misled into voting against their own interests. Love you
> Moe; don't be fooled.

Of course, it would never occur to that writer that she might be the one fooled. I mean, could it be that Moe realized how bereft of common sense hipster life was, and moved on? I'd bet a hamster that writer was over forty years old. Who cares? It's Moe who is misled. And therefore she is no longer part of the in crowd.

So where did the tolerance of "opposing viewpoints" go? Weren't artists supposed to be truly rebellious—meaning that they should also rebel against the status quo of the hipsters around them? Shouldn't they be admired for rejecting the litmus test? In short, music bloggers, aren't *you* the machine they should be raging against?

Nope. Apparently the lockstep liberal pop stars and their slavish followers must ensure that every single pop legend shares their oh-so-predictable worldview. If you don't, you're obviously misguided. This ostracism—intolerance from the self-proclaimed open-minded—is driven not by the coolness they believe only they possess but by a sheep mentality—something real rebels would openly mock.

Now, caution: we're about to enter a name-dropping zone.

As a former punker, I found nothing more glorious than when Johnny Rotten showed up to do my three AM show. This man, in my opinion, is the greatest rebel in modern music. The Sex Pistols created the singular antiestablishment record of their age— something that has never been repeated and probably never will be. No one, in my mind, was cooler than Rotten—he was smart, scary, and funny—and the songs were awesome. When he told me how much he enjoyed doing the show, I almost died. We went out drinking until the wee hours of the morning at a local Irish bar, and he told me how much he hates hippies and hipsters. I realized the guy I had posters of on my wall when I was in my teens felt like me. Don't get me wrong—I don't think Rotten was a conservative. I doubt he labels himself at all, and he really likes Obama. But I don't think he trafficked in the repressive tolerance that flourishes around him to this day. He just hates phonies.

When I drank beer with Billy Zoom, the legendary guitarist from the L.A. punk band X, and found a like-minded soul, I realized how cool "cool" really was. Zoom is a taciturn fellow whose stoic guitar stance transforms him into a far cooler icon than James Dean. This guy shits cool. And even his shit shits cool.

And he's about as liberal as Allen West. The same goes for Joe Escalante, who's been on my show many times. A founder of The Vandals, Escalante is both a punker and a bullfighter—but also a Catholic, and a God-fearing one at that. He's so punk that other punkers steer clear of him. I almost forgive him for being a bass player.

I am still a slave to pop culture. I listen to nothing but punk, metal, and obscure electronica. I watch weird movies in the middle of the night, and I continue to fight the war against hipster intolerance by persuading my favorite bands to come on my show. I'm pretty sure I helm the only show on any news cable channel to have Fucked Up, the essential Canadian punk band, as a guest. They're as left-wing as you can get, but I adore their music.

But in this war, I found a cohort in the battle—Gavin McInnes, the founder of *Vice* magazine, a subversive piece of filth that erupted in the nineties and became the hipster bible. But as a hipster, Gavin does not hold to the hipster code. He does not think Obama is a savior. And he hates big government. He's a conservative-leaning libertarian who thinks drugs should be legal and supports Occupy Wall Street—although at the same time condemning self-destructive stoners and anarchic violence. He writes frequently on the necessities of hard work, and how young adults these days are more interested in looking cool than actually "doing" cool things. He's covered in tattoos but raises his kids like a normal dad, and finds no pleasure in anyone denigrating others for being "weird." Gavin is a hipster, but he's also the hardest-working capitalist I know (I just wish he wouldn't strip so often in public). When I took him to an event for conservatives in the entertainment world, I joked about how nerdy it was. He frowned at me and said, "I've been around hip all my life. I'll take this over that. This is good." It's like he knew, instantly, what real noncomformity was—and it has nothing to do with tattoos, nose rings, or shouting "the world is watching" at cops. I felt bad that I was embarrassed.

Nobody got this more than Andrew Breitbart. It was his mission, in a way, to call bullshit on the whole facile notion of "cool" being the defining principle for adult behavior. Cool sucks. And Andy knew it. So does Gavin. And Johnny. And Billy. And that makes them way cooler than anyone else I knew, or know.

Among phony hipsters, tolerance for other people ends where their fear of real rebellion begins. "Hip" people who happen to be conservative tend to reject the stereotypical "hip" assumptions, and therefore are the least tolerated phenomenon you will find. According to the sheep with nose rings, you can't possibly love The Clash and have voted for Bush (I did). You can't possibly have seen Gang of Four and sung along to every song, then worked at *The American Spectator* (I did). There's no way you are obsessed with both the Melvins and Congressman Allen West (that's me). The fact is, these hipster weasels don't get those possibilities, because they reject real, authentic rebellion. The people they hate are truly *authentic* in their questioning, in their rebellion—and they are not.

And it's got to hurt them. I mean, imagine being a lefty rocker who adores X and finding that the guitarist, who is far cooler than you, thinks your politics stink. It's gotta fry your brain. No wonder you wear board shorts and wallet chains to the beer garden.

But the bigger and final message here is what happens when someone from The Velvet Underground—the band that Václav Havel credits for creating the Czech Republic (personally, I haven't been able to establish the link)—gets crap for showing up at a peaceful political event. And what does it mean when a member of the most naturally subversive band of the last forty years shows up at the most naturally subversive movement in recent memory?

By witnessing the shocked reaction, you see where true rebellion lurks.

It's wherever Moe's at.

And, really, how can you not follow someone named Moe?

FAT KIDS ARE THE BIGGEST TARGETS

AS PEOPLE STARVE ALL OVER THE GLOBE, we are demonizing chubby kids. Don't get me wrong, being fat is unhealthy, but last time I checked, fat kids weren't spreading disease, mugging the elderly, or beating the crap out of people on subways. At least, not as a general rule. There are a lot of bad eggs on this planet, but don't blame the kids who seem to be eating too many of them. Remember, the fatter they are, the harder it is for them to run from a crime. (It's why I went on Atkins.)

Repressive tolerance is a weak, weird thing. Like water, it flows along the path of least resistance. And apparently no one can stand a fat kid, so that's where the tolerant express their easy, lame intolerance. If a kid is fat, the most tolerant liberal has no trouble passing judgment, and perhaps a tax, to register their disapproval. In a world where you are expected to tolerate all behavior, somehow fat kids didn't get the note from Congress exempting them from condemnation. Fat kids are now a big target, and it has nothing to do with their big pants purchased at Target.

This intolerance toward the chubby means little until you compare it with other behaviors that are accepted, or even encouraged, among the community of tolerance.

In Georgia, a series of depressing anti-obesity ads created

controversy, according to the *New York Daily News,* because they featured unhappy fat kids talking about being fat. The ads offered messages like "Some diseases aren't just for adults anymore," and "Being fat takes the fun out of being a kid." (Which is untrue. If there's any time to be fat, it's when you're a kid and don't care about being attractive.) Children's Healthcare of Atlanta made the ads, intending their grim message to spark parents to see how serious this "epidemic" is. Here's a quote from Linda Matzigkeit, a senior vice president at Children's Healthcare:

> We felt like we needed a very arresting, abrupt campaign that said: "Hey Georgia! Wake up. This is a problem."

Hey Linda, here's an arresting campaign for you: you're the problem.

Yeah, okay—fat kids are a problem. But imagine for a second an ad campaign that features a provocatively dressed teen talking about how her/his sexual conquests have left her/him empty and unwanted. You can't, because it never happens.

Now, they might do the ad for the sexually active teen, in which they warn of consequences like STDs or unwanted pregnancies. But the fact is, they will never say *"Don't do it."* They won't say that, on a moral level, such behavior leaves you empty and used up, just as everyone else is discovering what you've already exhausted. The concerned just say use protection. In the upside-down world of tolerance, eating a sloppy joe is wrong, but screwing one is okay. Being tolerant means eating sugary food is evil, but anything in the bedroom is none of my business. Frankly, I don't care what you eat or who you screw, but please remain consistent in your condemnations of personal behavior. If you say, "Don't eat Big Macs," then you should just as easily say, "Don't do

Big Mac." (This is good advice: anyone named Big Mac is probably a long-haul trucker who's a bit rough in the sack.)

I don't give a damn what kids do, as long as they don't hurt me. And fat kids don't hurt me. However, violent kids do. We've seen a wild spurt of teenaged packs rumbling stores and subways. We've seen countless kids pregnant with kids—there's a show on MTV that has turned teen pregnancy into the Olympic trials for our sad, stupid culture. We've got a system that's spending crap-loads more than what we spent in the seventies on education, but producing dumber and dumber kids, who know little more than how to create texting abbreviations. We've got teachers, immune from the demands of discipline or competency thanks to unions, doing little more than monitoring classrooms like they're unruly ant farms, while surveying their student bodies for the best student body.

But what is the White House concerned about? Fat kids . . . the "epidemic" of fat kids. What horseshit. Look, all you have to know about the U.S. is one thing: each year a person born usually lives longer than a person born the previous year. So we are doing something right. A lot of that has to do with not starving to death. It's yet another Gutfeld scientific theory: available food = less starvation. I feel confident in this one.

But not tolerating fat people really is about not tolerating a fat, bloated America. When I lived in England, the joke was always how fat we Yanks were. It was like every bulging Bostonian was emblematic of a sweaty, heaving America. Look at us, eating our way to freedom, devouring Iraq and Afghanistan, while pooping out imperialism. Our jokes about British teeth were a jab at their medical services, but their jokes about our weight were a summary of our greedy lifestyle.

I guess that drives lean beans like Obama crazy. Why can't we be skinny, like those alluring Belgians! Sure, they do nothing for the world but produce artery-clogging chocolate, but they can buy their jeans at Gap Kids.

To Obama and the hard left, it's all a metaphor for the hated American exceptionalism. Truth is, if America is fatter than other nations, it's because we can be. Now, that doesn't make it desirable, for health reasons and for reasons related to the wearing of Speedos. But the reason this incites such a visceral reaction from the Kathleen Sebeliuses of the world is that it sets us apart as having a more successful economy than places where the people subsist on 120 calories a day. We've created a system so successful that the most universal problem in human history—the acquisition of foodstuffs—has been erased by the issue of having too much of them (only America pays farmers so much money not to grow food). For the Obamatrons out there, every time a fat kid eats a scooter pie, a child in The Hague cries. I blame Bush. The president and the baked beans.

Again, imagine if you mapped this same strategy for sexual activity—taking classes where you'd be credited, say, if you remained a virgin until graduation. Or only gave out two blow jobs, instead of, say, seven. That would never happen, because it's too judgmental, too intolerant, too intrusive. It's also a bit tougher to monitor, I'll admit, although I'm available if needed. More important, it doesn't agree with the wisdom received from that boxed set of *Sex and the City,* which dictates that casual sex makes you happy, smart, and successful. And the possessor of a bigger apartment than mine. (Hell, I'd sleep with Chris Noth too if I could get the kind of digs they had on that show.)

However, when it comes to edible things that you put in your mouth, that's different. This is why in school superintendents can tell you that a hot dog is a no-no at lunch, but in the sex ed class, it's okay if it wears a condom. I'm beginning to think sex ed is taught so teachers can make sure the students have condoms on when they run into them after class. I wonder: Would these teachers be okay with eating a hot dog if the kids slipped a condom on it?

Right now, in New York (geographically part of America), we've got a mayor who demonizes giant sodas. We have experts up the wazoo saying we should do the same with all fattening foods—their argument being that if fattening foods lead to fat people, who then greedily utilize more health care and thus are a burden on our society, then why shouldn't their greasy blubbery lifestyles be taxed?

Okay, then. Why not then tax sexually transmitted diseases? I venture the cost to society from sexual behavior has to be every bit as high as eating at McDonald's or Wendy's, so why aren't we "going there"? At least when I eat a Quarter Pounder, I'm not getting herpes from the Quarter Pounder (sadly, I can't say the same thing for the Quarter Pounder).

The ideas are the same: we are talking about behaviors in excess—eating too much and screwing too much. Both lead to bad places that present a cost to society, if not your own soul, if you have one (I do, I keep it in my sock drawer). Whether it's eating or banging, the flaw lies with self-control, in discipline—and how much we've devalued it since we lost the power to shame. However, one vice can be tolerated while another cannot. Why is that?

Well, it's not about sex or fatness, but about how America sucks. And fat people represent America, while sexual liberation represents the more tolerant, sophisticated Europe. Desperately, our media, academics, and politicians seek approval from those so far up that evolved food chain that we cannot risk looking prehistoric when it comes to sexuality. Saying yes to sex but no to food satisfies that insecurity: yes, we know we are fat, but we're not prudes.

Look, I know being fat isn't healthy. I was fat for a while, and it's no fun. I crowded every elevator (even when alone). My wife couldn't stand me. Mirrors reminded me that I gave up, every single day.

But on the list of things that shouldn't be tolerated, a chubby kid shouldn't even show up. A kid who, with other kids, crowds a store and pummels the clerk for kicks—or a kid who thinks getting pregnant is the only way to be somebody (or at least on MTV)—ranks far higher than a tyke who gains momentary pleasure from an innocent Twinkie. Or who, genetically, simply has that body type.

And let's not forget that when a successful actor or model is interviewed and their childhood is brought up, nearly all of them mention they were once fat. One could argue that nearly every husky kid inevitably grows up to be slim, fabulous, and famous. It's an argument that is not backed up by research, but that will not stop me from making its case.

In sum, I'd rather have a fat kid than a promiscuous kid. At least we can bake together.

THE SKEPTIC TANK

IF THERE'S ANYTHING THAT CAN KILL A PARTY, it's global warming. God, I hate the topic, only because I know *too* much about it. I wish I could take a toilet scrubber to my brain and clear out all that wasteful crap I've stuck in there simply because I felt I *had* to read about it. Actually, I had to read *up* on it. Because I just didn't buy the crap I was hearing on the news, and I had to find out why.

When I was cutting my gorgeous teeth writing health pieces for *Prevention* magazine, my life consisted of reading dozens of medical journals every month. It was boring, kinda like hanging out with Bill Nye the Science Guy. But I got the hang of the terminology, and figured out what were real results and what was conjecture. Or hype.

From this constant reading I knew the real results were to be found in a study's conclusion—not in a phony press release, exaggerated to get a headline, which would lead to more grants and more press.

That means when I got a press release that said, "clam smoothies doubled results of placebo," I knew to go straight to the numbers—who and how many people were used in the study—and then examine all the charts and graphs showing the results. How many got better? How many turned blue? How many, after treatment, were convinced they were wallabies?

And sure enough, that line about clam smoothies doubling results of placebo started to look less and less important. Apparently, from the actual study, it meant that instead of just one guy getting relief, now there were two—out of 1,000 patients.

Hence the "doubled" results. This crap happens all the time in health studies, and magazines love it because they can play along to sell copies. I mean, if you claim your crappy pill works, that makes a great cover line for the magazine, who will then sell copies based on your flimsy claim. "Double your weight loss!" sells copies, not "clam smoothies lead to positive results in two people instead of one, out of a thousand." Also, if you add a shot of my astounding abs, which are actually a henna tattoo, it helps.

Health is different from climate science, but the jargon and hysteria that follow are often the same. I learned early on that jargon is used to confuse and overwhelm you, so you're more likely to agree with whoever is spewing the nonsense just to shut them up. Jargon is also great for hiding incompetence and corruption: You're less likely to question motives or skill if you're reeling from all those multisyllabic Latinate words. Especially when they're *italicized.*

I learned to get around this crap by asking doctors (in my many, many awkward interviews) very simple questions, and admitting right off the bat that I'm a moron. I would say, "Hey, I was an English major in college, so what exactly is a blood vessel?" The doctors quickly took me for an idiot (which saved time), but also found my idiotic honesty refreshing, and they walked me through the stuff that other reporters chose not to pursue. This is exactly how I cured my psoriasis. (Kidding—I don't have psoriasis. Psoriasis isn't purple, is it?)

Once I walked myself through the research and talked it through with its authors, I often came to a very basic conclusion: no one knows what the hell they're talking about. I mean, even with the drugs that do work, most experts are not even sure why. And now, with so much evidence lauding the work of antidepressants, there's a whole band of critics who say that's baloney. And it turns out the best doctors are the ones who bend over backwards to say they don't know crap. Every one in the medical field looks down at MDs who blow their own horn. They see them as hucksters.

And so I learned a key skill—to steer clear of anyone who can announce with any certainty that they know the future. I don't care how smart the scientist is, they're almost always wrong. Remember that jackass in the seventies who predicted the coming ice age? Or how about that other dope who predicted global starvation? I venture both of them are dead, so they don't have to answer for their asinine predictions. But there were many like them—people who could predict with all certainty that the world was going to end. And get this: it's *your fault*. This kind of crap sold books and got grants and guaranteed tenure for many people, all of whom really should have been kicked out on their keisters and forced to get a real job like everyone else.

Examples abound. You remember the radon gas scare? We were told by America's newsweeklies (back when their circulation was greater than that of a free pamphlet on osteoarthritis) that the scourge of radon gas collecting at the base of America's homes would lead to all sorts of horrors—most specifically, an explosion of lung cancer. Hasn't happened. The basic premise was that radon gas, which occurs naturally, would collect at unnaturally dense levels in our homes and begin killing us systematically. A whole radon-mitigation industry germinated. Then, finally!

Cooler heads in the scientific world pushed back on the alarmists peddling this stuff for fun and profit (among them, the EPA), and the radon gas threat dissipated like . . . radon gas. But understand: Somebody—most likely someone with a specious PhD, a white lab coat, and a good sales pitch—enhanced his career and bank account significantly from this twaddle (thanks for that word, O'Reilly).

My point is, when someone says something dire is going to happen—whether it's an ice age, global warming, or the death of polka music—put on goggles because you're about to be hit in the face with a pile of crap. They've been predicting the death of the polka for years, and like the sun, it's still here every day. I play it very loud, every single morning. My neighbors love it!

So because of my own experience in health journalism, I've always cast a skeptical eye toward exaggerated claims of global warming—or whatever you might call it these days, since that moniker has changed. We call it climate change now. In a few years, what will we call it? Weather variability? Manic meteorology? Who cares? Whatever it's called, it will make no more sense than it does now. And my eyes will still be skeptical.

Which is why I read as much as I can on the issue, choosing papers from both sides (which, you'll later find, is now considered heresy in the eyes of scientists who are intolerant of any skeptical point of view).

My conclusion is that, for the most part, a lot of the climate change journalism is misinformed, exaggerated, and crap. Having said that, I'll just add: who knows—maybe something is happening. I mean, something is always happening around us that we can't explain. I've got the strangest rash on my leg that looks like William F. Buckley. Is that global warming? Or the fact that I slept in a hedge last night? This is why I keep an open mind about this sort of stuff, and you should, too.

But an open mind is not enough. Apparently. A few years back, I had a guy on my late-night show, and the topic was global warming. The chap was a friend of mine and he had e-mailed me three times to ask to come on the show. So I figured, why not? I'm tolerant like that. And considering the hosts, we set the bar for guests at a fairly, er, accommodating level.

During the segment on global warming, however, he did something that only the repressive tolerati do when faced with something that undermines their worldview. He got personal.

I asked him, and I paraphrase it, because it was a while ago and before the hypnosis treatments, "What's wrong with hearing two sides of the debate on climate change?" He replied, and I paraphrase again, "Who would I want to believe, the hundreds of scientists who have studied this phenomenon, or some guy who hosts a show in the middle of the night?"

Ouch. I was wounded. And all I did was ask a question, but it was a question, apparently, that should never be asked: What would be wrong with looking at both sides of a debate? He dismissed my simple question about balanced reporting by pointing out that, as a late-night talking boob with a crease in my forehead, I'm not equipped to entertain such lofty thoughts. Sensing, however, a salient point to be made, I replied, "Okay, well let me ask you this: Who would you rather listen to, a guy who hosts a show in the middle of the night or some guy who e-mailed him a million times to get on the show, you douchebag?"

I probably didn't need to call him a douchebag, but he deserved it. He had asked me if he could be on the show, and being the tolerant lad that I am, I said yes to a well-meaning liberal. But in a world where every good liberal says you're supposed to tolerate both sides of a debate, global warming is exempt from that principle, as are many other topics, and if you express any uncertainty at all (which is the mark of a good scientist), you're considered an idiot. Especially some moron who hosts a show in the middle of the night.

Quick aside on this "uncertainty" idea: When Einstein (who I'm pretty sure was a scientist) formulated his first theory of relativity, it was ultimately greeted with universal acclaim by all the eggheads. They were stunned by it—it pushed Western science ahead by several orders of magnitude, and with formulas that were, at that level of science, fairly simple and straightforward. As other scientists subjected it to the proper adversarial peer review and found it be holding up, the first theory of relativity became a scientific phenomenon. Only one person had serious doubts about it: this guy named Einstein. Who later published his second (general) theory of relativity, expanding on his first significantly and again stunning the scientific world, which proves that first, good scientists doubt, and second, that I just Googled "Albert Einstein."

He proved a point, however: The left will tolerate any balanced approach toward the most insidious ideas, but when it comes to spending hundreds of billions of your money on hypotheticals, they're, like, sure, why not? Because it makes them feel smart, and you look dumb. Better to throw billions at something we can't put our finger on than build the Keystone XL oil pipeline, which actually creates jobs and delivers fuel from Canada, a country we actually get along with.

And that's where the climate change debate, mitigated by repressive tolerance, finally rests. There is no debate, and there is no tolerance for those who consider otherwise—even if science always reminds us nothing is absolute. Nothing. Remember when we thought dolphins couldn't talk? Yeah, then we saw a show called *Flipper.*

So what happens if you decide to cover climate change more diligently than your peers? What if you try to present both sides of the debate because you figure it's better than blindly saying, "Yeah, what he said"? You'd think that would be lauded as an example of supreme tolerance, right? Not so fast, you flat-earther (those are Obama's words). According to a new study by something called the *International Journal of Press/Politics* (it's a publication and a laundromat), providing balanced coverage means you're actually super biased because you're giving climate change critics a larger voice.

So let's get this straight: Because other media outlets refuse to show both sides, you are biased when you actually try to promote balance. I'm not sure even Einstein could devise an equation that makes sense of that.

This journal looked at how Fox News, CNN, and MSNBC (the lemonade stand with more hosts than viewers) covered global warming, and concluded that while Fox News covered the issue roughly twice as much as the other networks *combined,* it was just not a good thing—because their coverage was just . . . too . . . mean!

According to the study researchers, from an article in *U.S. News & World Report,* "Although Fox discussed climate change most often, the tone of its coverage was disproportionately dismissive." They added, "Fox broadcasts were more likely to include statements that challenged the scientific agreement on climate change, undermined the reality of climate change, and questioned its human causes." Yikes! Fox challenged, undermined, and questioned! To the gallows!

That quote, right there, shows you that tolerance is not deemed necessary if you reformat the game board so anyone who questions the basic assumptions is disqualified from playing. In order to report on climate change, you must first already accept their version of climate change—and accept all of their assumptions about the "science." Perhaps they will end up correct in their preformed conclusions, but to say it might be fun to debate that idea—well, that's incorrect. That's not science at all. It's something else. Oh yeah. It's asinine.

The report says that Fox News tended more toward the "critic" side than the "proponent" side, but in my opinion that is BS. Something tells me that any opinion that deviates from the proponent point of view will be disregarded as "disproportionately dismissive." If you don't blindly swallow the climate change pill whole, and agree to spending hundreds of billions of dollars of your cash, then you're just not to be taken seriously. And you're biased.

How funny that nearly all these apostles for global warming mock those who believe in a higher being. How stupid is it to cling to something you can't prove? Well, maybe that's why they cling so desperately to climate change. It has become their religion, replacing the gaping maw in their own life that something more substantial was meant to fill. Like God. Or pilates.

It's probably something else. A need for some kind of directed outrage—a place to park your intolerance. Like cigarette smoking, climate change skepticism is an easy and acceptable target for those seeking to exercise their intolerant muscles. These muscles, so atrophied from years of accepting everyone in the fold, need a workout. They need someone to headlock. The tolerati seek skeptics as targets because, in effect, they're bullies seeking release. And worse, they are cowardly bullies, in that they only go after the sanctioned targets.

So I guess it's just better not to talk about it. Frankly, it bores the hell out of everyone in the room. And face it, there are bigger things to worry about. For example, global cooling is apparently on its way—temporarily, before we get hit with more global warming. And then, after that, it's back to cooling again. Some might even say we're probably going to see some sort of "ice age," although that might have been a Nordic male stripper I met last night in line at Port Authority. He needed a place to crash.

But what happens if you're a normal guy who has a change of heart about global warming? What if you go from apostle to apostate? You become a delightful gentleman named Harold Ambler. If you don't know Harold, you should. Harold is an editor/writer who's worked at all the right places, including *The New Yorker,* and does all the right things. He's a singer in a band, he's a rower, he runs his own blog, and by all accounts he's a liberal. If you needed a charming, good-looking person to star in one of those commercials for the *New York Times* Sunday edition, he'd be there—probably wearing a denim shirt with an Obama Hope and Change button in plain view. But there's a problem with Harold. As cool and edgy as he sounds, he's really a leper—a man who chose his own leprosy, by voicing skepticism regarding climate change.

A few years back the Huffington Post was looking for someone to blog (for free, of course) about climate change, and Ambler was recommended. A self-taught expert on climate, he ran a witty website about all things weather. He e-mailed Arianna several times. Arianna was receptive (as she always is to free writing), and cc'd an editor to "coordinate" with Harold. The piece got published, and it garnered a huge amount of attention—for the wrong reasons. Ambler had trashed every left-wing notion of climate change. It was two days later that Arianna disowned

Harold—and said that he was published without her absolute knowledge. She made it clear that climate change was a subject where dissent could not be tolerated.

How did he respond to the intolerance of the tolerant? "The treatment I received at the hands of various U.S. leftists at the time removed the scales from my eyes somewhat about how groovy these supposed hippies were. I found Arianna herself and her henchmen, and others I've run into since on the Internet, to be pernicious bullies interested in accruing power for themselves and their brethren and more or less totally out of touch with regular people." Harold, where have you been all my life?

And for those of you who think Harold's just a skeptic for the sake of being different, the fact is, he's read more about about the science than most of the folks who make a real living off climate change. He's read scores of scientific articles and books, and interviewed scientists as well. He's beyond articulate on the cosmic-ray theory of cloud production—something we'll leave for my next book, *The Cosmic-Ray Theory of Cloud Production.* In short, he knows his shit. He knew it enough for Arianna to hire him. "I understand why people would be concerned . . . but it turns out carbon dioxide is just a lot less powerful than most regular folk have been led to believe." And he makes the simple point that the planet has been warmer than today, dozens and dozens of times in the past, without a single SUV in existence. Mentioning that, however, will not be tolerated in places like the Huffington Post. "If you tell them that we've been cooling since 6,000 years ago, they get offended because it messes with their narrative. How dare you bring that up?"

And that really is how repressive tolerance works. Intolerance springs into action whenever their assumptions are threatened by facts. It's the equivalent of plugging your ears with your fingers and humming loudly. Even better, by claiming that everything can be linked to global warming (rainstorms, windstorms, snowstorms, Hannah Storm), a skeptic becomes the heretic for not seeing the threat that's right in front of his ignorant eyeballs.

Hatred toward skepticism also arises from another dark and dreary place: the human ego, which is in no short supply among the liberal left. "People living in the early twenty-first century want to believe they are living in a special time, being special people," says Ambler. "This is a matter of profound religious faith that has come to dominate the sphere of Western media to an astonishing extent." Because it makes you feel important: not only is the world in peril, but you can do something to stop it. And anyone standing in between you and that goal must not be tolerated. "It's witch-burning all over again," says Ambler. Maybe that's what instigated global warming—all those witch-burnings way back when!

And what do you do with witches? "A Canadian blogger recently said in a discussion in which I'd had the audacity to bring up a few facts that maybe someone might want to burn down Harold Ambler's house," says Harold. "I looked into prosecuting him for hate speech, seriously, but it didn't seem worth the effort. But it was Christmastime when he said it, and it didn't add to my sense of the season!"

Where does this leave the heretic? "I can't comfortably describe myself as a liberal anymore. The nearest thing I might be able to convey in terms of where my politics are now is something that I say all the time: I'm a man without a country."

The good news is, wherever you are, it will be delightfully cooler than anywhere else.

WOOLLY BULLIES

THIS JUST IN: Bullying sucks. I know this—not from common sense—but from the tidal wave of talking heads telling me it sucks. It's like I'm being bullied into admitting bullying is wrong. For example, I recently received a press release, sent to me by a PR flack trying to get her client on my show. The client is an "anti-bullying" expert, which puts her in a pool of about 4 billion people claiming to be anti-bullying experts. The gist of the release: Bullying is an extreme version of intolerance, and intolerance is an extreme version of bullying. I really didn't read the whole thing—I was too busy beating up someone less fortunate than me (my stunted half-brother Gunnar).

But this all fits nicely into the world of modern grievance: If you ignore the laws of tolerance, or do not bend to the cries of manufactured outrage, then you run the risk of being called something supremely horrible: a bully. I'm used to it.

Yep, if you do not express the required amount of sympathy for something you hardly care about, then clearly you are mean. And if you're mean, you're a bully. You never have to lift a finger or call someone a nasty name. Just saying anything considered disagreeable by the powers that be makes you a bully. And that makes you a cash cow for experts who make money off this sudden bullying epidemic.

Let's focus on the anti-bullying crusade that's sweeping the country. From high schools to the White House, the topic of bullying has elbowed its way to the front of the grievance parade. City councils are passing "anti-bullying laws," and the term is now used to describe all sorts of bad behavior. The movie *Bully* is making big news as I cobble these words together, for it is a controversial, sobering look at what many people call a frightening trend. I haven't seen the flick. I prefer German art films, but you can't get them here anymore after the crackdown.

And of course there is a bigger picture here. America is always accused of being the world's bully, despite the crap we take from just about everyone. Because America is bigger, we are naturally the target of blame—even if the tiny countries we're dealing with are jerks. The UN operates on the assumption that America is a bully, which is why we continue to subsidize that awful enterprise. The only way to get out of being called a bully is to agree with the tolerati's assumptions about your own innate bullying. Like I said, you are bullied into being a bully.

To overuse a cliché, size matters. In my life, I've rarely met large men who were bullies. Sure, there were assholes on the football team, but they generally kept to their asshole selves. But take someone the size of genius magician Penn Jillette—who, I would guess, is about eleven feet tall. I come up to his shoelaces. What he told me about bullying, however, is something I pretty much knew already (as a little guy): It's often the big guys who get bullied most, because their size prevents them from fighting back. A little shrimp like me can taunt Penn all I want, and if he strikes me, I get the sympathy—and he looks like a big bad bully. So he has to take it, and I get to look cool for picking on someone whose front pocket I could sleep in.

My point: Penn Jillette is America, and Iran (or Cuba, or Venezuela) is me.

So why has the anti-bullying movement become so popular among the tolerati? Well, it's an easy thing to get earnest about: no matter how much of a jerk you are (and I'm at the top), you can't say, "Bullying is awesome." You can say it builds character, but don't tell that to a parent of a terrified kid.

But it's also a cause célèbre for your assorted mid-level celebrities looking for a leg up in their faltering careers. It makes for legitimate, you-build-it outrage that even the shallowest dope can get behind, because it requires a minimum of vocabulary ("bullying is bad" is all a typical starlet might have to say, if she were sober long enough to say it). It kills me, however, that nearly all celebrities fit the bullying profile, especially when you get between them and their goody bag at an awards show. In fact, many of these idiots got into show business so they could establish bullying as a lifestyle—they hire people specifically to yell at other people. That guy telling you "it gets better" in a PSA ad was just moments ago throwing a Naugahyde sandal at his hapless Senegalese driver. For the driver, it only "gets worse." It may also get "weird." It often gets "uncomfortable" and "disgusting." It may even become "actionable." But it never "gets better."

What is most laughable, however, is how every celebrity prepares for that talk show or magazine interview moment when they must remind us that they were once bullied too (which seems to me to be an argument *for* bullying—it's the keystone of success!). The anti-bullying cause becomes about their own personal expression of inner torment, just like everything else does. So my guess is, they have recast their past to where now, looking back, they're the ones who got ridiculed in the hallways of their high school, instead of the other way around.

And this leads me to a simple discovery: There's a bully gap going on. Everyone claims to be bullied. No one claims to be the bully. Ever.

Look, I was bullied once. His name was Patrick. And he was a bona fide moron, who would sometimes force me to let him cheat off me (this happens a lot when you're a good student who wants to keep his teeth). During one summer, he followed me home daily, demanding money from me. When I finally stood up to him, he sulked off convinced, no doubt, that I'd bullied *him*.

So I guess everyone on the planet was bullied. I'm betting you were bullied, too. Which leads me to my only question: If we were all bullied, where are the bullies?

The answer: We're both. We can be bullied and bullies. I remember being bullied, yep. But if I try harder, I can also remember Spanish class at Serra High. The teacher's name was Mr. Fojo, a Cuban refugee. He went through hell to make it here, and I made it worse. Sorry, Mr. Fojo. I know he's no longer on this earth, but I remember the crap I pulled in his class (surrounding his podium with snails, on which he slipped), and now it makes me feel sick to my stomach. That's what an honest memory does: it tells you truths about yourself you'd rather not know. Sort of like a wife you've had since childhood.

So perhaps I should start some sort of special grievance group— made up of former bullies. We can all come forward and talk about the guilt we carry for being a jerk. Perhaps if I make it acceptable to confess, and turn it into a badge of victimhood like everything else in life, this bully gap will disappear.

At any rate, in the world of the manufactured grievance industry, the bully card will be played more and more—as yet another effective and insidious weapon in the arsenal designed to force you into an enhanced realm of tolerance. Remember, if you're against

Obamacare, you must be cruel. If you won't pay for Sandra Fluke's birth control pills, you're heartless. If you talk about immigration without linking it to full-on amnesty, you're a really mean person. If you vote Republican, you hate the poor—and therefore are the worst kind of bully.

So yeah, I must say that bullying is wrong. But only when it's real. But the way it is bandied about now, like an amorphous emotional version of chronic fatigue syndrome, it's as fake as your recovered memories of victimhood. The world is a churning mess of emotional responses, thoughtless actions, mean people. But it'll only "get better" if we admit most of it dissipates like memories of the flu. And that we gave as good as we got.

THE BARD OF BRENTWOOD

TO SAY I MISS ANDREW BREITBART is an understatement. It's like saying I miss my left arm, if I'd actually lost it. Breitbart took great joy in tying the tentacles of phony tolerance into knots. Whereas tolerance demanded that you accept everything, including crap that could destroy you, one thing the tolerance patrol could not tolerate was this wonderful thing called Andrew Breitbart.

He confused them. He was a cross between a Sudoku puzzle and anthrax—complicated and deadly—and all wrapped in a lazy California accent and projected from a set of eyes that anyone could see would not be intimidated.

He was fiercely conservative and fiercely funny—which, for the left, is simply unacceptable. He was highly moral but deeply twisted—a Reese's Peanut Butter Cup that proved poisonous to adversaries. He was a patriot and a prankster—and according to mainstream "wisdom," only people like Michael Moore or Abbie Hoffman could be like that. He was dead serious about his mission, but funnier than most comedians who've worked decades on their "craft."

It was why, with such zeal, the left tried to silence Andrew through harassment and threats. Andrew first and foremost understood the Internet, and the power of the social media, having worked on Drudge, helped launch the Huffington Post (where we met), and then created his own media empire, Big Hollywood, Big Government, Big Journalism, and so on. (He came up with the "big" idea as a play on the left's constant demonization of things they did not understand or like by calling them Big this or that.) When Andrew came to Twitter, he was hammered by thousands of sordid threats, and he would often retweet them with glee, an exercise designed to show how intolerant the so-called tolerant progressives are. Breitbart found the whole thing hilarious, even if his Twitter followers didn't. They didn't get Andrew's mission, which was to drive the left batty and watch the battiness express itself through sheer, bloodcurdling intolerance. For some, the anger and vitriol were sickening. For Andrew, it was pure comedy gold. Even the death threats he found delightful.

Andrew, like me, was one of the few regular targets of liberal bile who would receive two contradictory insults. Andrew could be labeled a "faggot" and a "homophobe," sometimes by the same red-faced progressive, who could get away with such slurs because leftists excuse homophobia as long as you're pro-gay! The reason for this dizzying slur also happened to be a high compliment: Andrew was straight and pro-gay—but more than anything he hated identity politics. For the left-wing gay activist, it undermined their reason for existing. If someone went up to Andrew and declared that he/she was proud to be a transgendered sex worker activist with dyslexia, he would say, "So?"

As Gavin McInnes has pointed out, "So" was Andrew's simplest and most cogent retort to the angry tolerance merchant. And one that usually left the ranters in sputtering silence.

The homophobic attacks on Andrew (oftentimes from gays) proved how intolerant the left could be when faced with arguments it could not handle. Calling him a "fag" was their white flag.

When he worked at the Huffington Post, and I was writing my progressive-mocking blogs there, I had created a fictitious roommate named Scott, who was a flight attendant, and I would allude to our relationship in a way that often devolved into the mysteriously perverse. I performed this exercise to see how the armies of tolerance would deal with me, when, predictably, they didn't like my ideas. Since many of them were clueless enough not to see that Scott was a fake, they would resort to calling me a homosexual (in varying degrees of intensity). Andrew and I loved it, for it exposed how phony their acceptance really was. If you didn't accept that America was at the root of all that was wrong in the world, then you must be a stupid, fat faggot (their words). At the time I was fat.

Andrew was a professional at exposing hypocrisy on the left, delighting in peeling back their manufactured compassion to reveal the angry, envious types that lurked beneath. He didn't hate them, he just found them fascinating—the way a child turns over a rock in a creek bed. In the battle against manufactured rage, Andrew was the tip of the spear. And in his death, that spear probably got sharper. Because Andrew, by inspiring so many people during his life, is all around us in his death. In a peculiar way, Andrew's death was like the Big Bang. Through his own spectacularly sudden demise, he sent particles of life in every single direction, creating new pockets of Andrews everywhere.

After Breitbart died, there was the predictable lefty dancing on his grave—in blog posts, on Twitter, in well-paid magazine articles. These crass exercises were condemned by the right, but something tells me Breitbart would have loved it. Their loathsome behavior was exactly how a beaten foe responds when their enemy exits. Their tackiness reflected how deeply Breitbart had wounded them with his insightful humor and invective. When that douchebag Matt Yglesias tweeted that the "world outlook is slightly improved with @andrewbreitbart dead," he only meant it was better for Matt Yglesias. Because there was one less person on the earth who could point out what a douchebag Matt Yglesias is.

Anyway, I wanted Breitbart to write a blurb for this book, and I'm still waiting to hear back. I'm still not sure he's dead.

THE END OF HATE

I hate book conclusions—they always seem so final. But it seems wrong to rail against phony outrage and the PC police without offering ways to combat both.

The first attack against manufactured anger: discerning the difference between real injustice and trumped-up baloney so you don't waste your time being pissed, which is time better spent thinking of ways to make your humble author happier.

The most obvious advice for everyone involved would be to lighten up. Get a thick skin. If someone says something that "offends" you, step back for a moment, and go through a mental checklist. Ask

Am I really offended? (Maybe . . . but if you're not sure, continue.)

Why am I angry then?

Is it because I like the person/issue/idea that the offender has targeted?

Is it because I don't like the offender in general?

Is it both? (It is.)

A few months ago, I came up with something called the Mirror Jerk Effect. This is how it works: Let's say Ed Schultz makes a crack about Sarah Palin that I don't like, because I like Palin and I don't like Schultz. I create a mirror effect. I say to myself, *What if, instead of Schultz and Palin, it's Rush and Garofalo?* If I don't care about Rush's opinion of a silly lefty, then I shouldn't care about a lefty's opinion of a conservative I like. This little mental exercise eliminates so much wasted energy that I now have time to help the poor and needy (i.e., myself).

For the most part you gotta think like one of those lions on the Serengeti, which I believe is in Canada. Conserve energy and then expend it when you need it most. Responding to every stupid remark or caustic joke will wear you down. That's why bitter people look decades older than they really are. I'm told Ed Schultz is actually twenty-six.

When does getting angry matter most? Well, when whatever is said is a threat to you, your family, your career. If someone says he's going to burn down your house, I think you have every reason to be concerned.

Also, when what the person says is not an opinion, but a lie. And it's a lie about someone you actually know. It could be about someone you admire, but I'd still hold back on that. Rush is better at defending Rush than I am. And he can do it in a twenty-million-dollar home in Florida. I have other things to worry about in my tiny Manhattan apartment. (The fumigation didn't take.)

But how about if what the person says is not a joke but a vicious attack. Look, I can disagree with Maher about his opinions on Palin, but I won't get angry about it. If, however, some weirdo starts getting creepy—imagining a person raped or whatever—then that's different. If you can't see the difference, then you are hopeless. But maybe it's better just to condemn them and move on. I hate that Mike Tyson is now a cuddly character. But what can I do about that? Nothing—other than to point it out.

Bottom line: 98 percent of the crap floating around in this world is not worth your time. What's worth your time? Your family, your friends, your work, my books. Sadly the world wide web has robbed major time from our lives, preventing us from actual conversation with people—actual people! Instead we allow perverse comments on a blog to cloud our minds, as if they actually mean something (and they don't, ever).

And another thing: Even if left-wing "watchdog" bozos like Media Matters do it, that doesn't mean you have to do it. Meaning, stop demanding that people shut up or get fired. We live in a country where you can say what you want. If you get fired, so be it. That's the call of the boss. But demanding that someone get fired because they hurt your feelings says more about you than them. You should not care. Generally, over time, creepy people end up creeping off into the sunset. See Olbermann. His bitter diatribes finally became his "thing," and it was a thing no one needed anymore. There is justice in the world, and for Olbermann, it's called obscurity.

So, forget about it. All of it. You are on this planet, if you are lucky, for seventy to ninety years. You won't be on your death bed remembering those things Maher said about whomever. They certainly won't be thinking of you when they start walking toward that bright light. Nope, you remember only the experiences with real people, not the fleeting emotional orgasm that is momentary outrage. You won't be lying there, thinking, "If only I crafted a better comment on that *HotAir* blog about Alec Baldwin. I really let myself down."

No, you'll be thinking of your kids. Your grandkids. My chiseled abs.

So there is no joy in hate. It's not worth it. Get out of the outrage pool, and into the party. It's more fun, and you won't get an infection.

THANKS 'N' STUFF

Writing a book while holding down a full-time job doing two one-hour shows is impossible without support from family, friends, alcohol, and prescription medications: So I'd like to thank all of them. Of course, I must thank my wife, again, who was very patient to put up with my mood swings, driven by bouts of combination editing/writing/drinking that would leave me dazed on the couch spouting gibberish. Thanks to my mom, as always, for producing me. Now, work-wise—a special thanks to the *Red Eye* crew and the malcontents at *The Five*. On both shows, I've been exploring the themes, rants, and ideas found in this book, and some of these chapters began as fifty-second monologues, often proofread by Dana Perino before the show. And I owe her so much. Despite what you hear, she's really a swell person. So is her husband, Peter. Everyone on *The Five*—Bob, Eric, Kimberly, Juan, and Andrea—have been a pleasure to be around, as well as all the producers (John, Porter, and the rest of the supportive crew). As for *Red Eye,* I thank them for putting up with me during a crazy period of work. It's the funnest job and a great crew (Andy, Bill, Todd, Ben, Tom, etc.) to work with.

Also thanks to Roger Ailes and everyone else at the evil Death

Star known as Fox News. It's the most exciting, interesting place to work, filled with great people and ridiculously hard workers. I thank, in no order: Sean Desmond, Jay Mandel, Paul Mauro, Gavin McInnes, Penn Jilette, Larry Gatlin, the ghost of Andrew Breitbart, Ann Coulter, Woody Fraser, Joanne McNaughton, and Wes. Also John Rich, Dennis Miller, Billy Zoom, Andrew Wu, Jack Wright, Gary Sinise, Robert Davi, Skunk Baxter, Bob Tyrell, Andy Ferguson, Matt Labash, Fabio, Carrot Top, Ginger Wildheart, John Moody, Jim Norton, Tom Shillue, and Dana Vachon. Also thanks to Dianne Brandi for her invaluable advice. Thanks to Aric Webb, who offered great insight into this book's concept. Mauro read it twice, killing my lame jokes, and adding some that were lamer. Thanks to all the local bars in my area who allowed me a corner in their taverns to slog through my piles of words—primarily Amarone, the West Side Steakhouse, Hallo Berlin—in order to carve out this book. Thanks to the local massage parlor. Thanks to Dr. Siegel. Thanks to Tobacco—the band and the substance. Also Torche and Tilts. Thanks to President Barack Obama for loaning me his collection of poetry when times got tough. And most of all, thank you, precious reader, for taking the time to indulge in my silly thoughts and mutant meanderings. I hope you are happy with your decision. Or drunk.

ABOUT THE AUTHOR

Greg Gutfeld is the author of five books and the host and cohost of two Fox News shows, *The Five* and *Red Eye*. He is married and lives in New York with his dwarf unicorn, Captain Hornface. He is triple-jointed and can bench press twice his own weight.